PRAISE FOR THE P~~OWER IN THE~~ PIVOT

"The Power in the Pivot is a testimony to the resilience of the human spirit—it's an engaging and inspiring read. Rich with honest conversations about the workplace, this book illustrates the capacity everyone has to turn challenge into opportunity. Andrea Butcher weaves these real stories together and extracts from them valuable and practical lessons that can make life at work more meaningful and fulfilling."

— JIM KOUZES, CO-AUTHOR OF AWARD-WINNING AND BEST-SELLING BOOK, THE LEADERSHIP CHALLENGE

"Achieving the impossible begins with doing the do-able. And Andrea Butcher shows you how through stories, strategies and self-reflective questions. A must read for every leader!"

— KAREN MANGIA, WALL STREET JOURNAL BEST SELLING AUTHOR AND SALESFORCE EXECUTIVE

"In The Power In The Pivot, Andrea Butcher distills common leadership themes shared by diverse entrepreneurs, athletes, HR pros, financial and tech experts, sales and marketing consultants and emerging leaders. Weaving in her own personal stories and leadership lessons, she provides authentic narratives, practical takeaways, and relatable perspectives that any leader and professional will find valuable. Her confident, caring, and calm approach to self-awareness and growth inspires me and will inspire others."

— KAREN ALTER, CEO, PARTNER AT BORSHOFF

"Andrea Butcher hits the mark with The Power in the PIVOT. I really loved the way she intertwined her story and key relationships with the leadership lessons learned from the guests of the first year of her leadership podcast, Being [at Work]. If you enjoy learning from transparent and raw stories with real life application, then this book is for you."

— KENT KRAMER, PRESIDENT AND CEO, GOODWILL OF
CENTRAL & SOUTHERN INDIANA

"The Power of the Pivot is a great read for any leader who wants to hear from real practitioners who are doing the work, giving concrete examples on how to bring your leadership practices to life. I think you will find the coaching questions at the end of chapter as a way to help you translate the concepts into real-world application."

— ADAM WEBER, SVP OF COMMUNITY AT 15FIVE

"Andrea takes a different and refreshing approach in THE POWER IN THE PIVOT from any leadership or management book I've ever read. Instead of an entire book espousing her views on "five easy steps," she presents insights, successes, failures and lessons learned from over 50 successful leaders. Drawn from episodes of her podcast, Being [at Work], these leaders talk about real world, relatable examples of various aspects of leadership. Andrea weaves in her own stories — career and personal experiences with leadership challenges throughout. She then challenges the reader with questions to get you thinking about your own career journey. In all, THE POWER IN THE PIVOT is a fantastic adventure!"

— KEVIN BRINEGAR, PRESIDENT AND CEO, INDIANA
CHAMBER OF COMMERCE

"Andrea, through real-life storytelling, has managed to capture the hardest lessons to learn as a leader and provide real answers to them. She shares her professional and personal moments of leadership from a unique perspective and inspires us to dig deep on leadership."

— JIM PIAZZA, DIRECTOR OF DATACENTER
OPERATIONS AT FACEBOOK

"Full of wisdom and poignant life lessons that transcend the business world. Andrea enables her guests to unpack pivotal professional experiences that have reshaped how these seasoned executives have come to understand themselves and what makes them impactful leaders within a chaotic world. Insightful, discerning and deep - this book captures the essence of personal discovery and a yearning for professional growth that is the foundation of all prodigious leaders."

— TREY WILLIS, CHIEF TECHNOLOGY OFFICER AT CTSI-
GLOBAL

This is masterful work pulling together lessons, stories, and *pivots* from a multitude of leaders. If you are on a path of continuous improvement, this is an easy read full of personal stories with actionable takeaways.

— MATT ODUM, PRESIDENT, BRILJENT

This book is simply amazing. The nuggets of wisdom from a diverse array of leaders combined with Andrea's personal stories of her experiences as a mother, wife, and business owner enlighten the reader to cultivate the spirit within, to never forsake the people we meet on the journey and trust ourselves along the way!

— TAMMY BUTLER, CEO, ENGAGING SOLUTIONS

Andrea's innovative launch of the podcast *Being [At Work]* being summarized in print is brilliant. She makes available a vast array of leadership experiences followed by simple questions to facilitate personal learning and application. A frontline Leader or Executive Leader is provided cogent thought and concise, provocative questions enabling thoughtful application. This is both a fun read and experiential lexicon.

— PHILIP MANN, SR. DIRECTOR, FACILITY LEADER,
MACY'S, INC.

A joy to read, with beautiful lessons for life and career packed into relatable stories and anecdotes. Andrea is a thoughtful, authentic, courageous leader, and her energy and humanity shine through in this book.

— KATE MAXWELL, CHIEF TECHNOLOGY OFFICER,
DEFENSE & INTELLIGENCE, MICROSOFT

THE POWER IN THE PIVOT

LEADERSHIP LESSONS FROM BEING [AT WORK]

FIRST EDITION (STORIES FROM YEAR 1 OF THE PODCAST)

ANDREA BUTCHER

Write to info@redthreadbooks.com if you are interested in publishing with Red Thread Publishing. Learn more about publications or foreign rights acquisitions of our catalogue of books: www.redthreadbooks.com

Paperback ISBN : 978-1-955683-30-2

Ebook ISBN : 978-1-955683-29-6

CONTENTS

This book is dedicated to my daughter, Mayson Moore, who has been my greatest source of inspiration and growth as a leader. Thank you, Mayson, for "staying on the stage" in all aspects of your life. The world needs more of you!

FOREWORD

Andrea Butcher and I share a passion for developing emerging leaders —we know through our own experiences that leadership is messy and hard. We know that it takes courage to step up and step out, so we are both continually encouraging early career leaders and new leaders.

When we first met, I was serving as a panelist for an event that Andrea hosted as part of a skill development program for emerging HR leaders. We were focusing on the partnership between HR and the c-suite, and the primary sentiment shared by all in the room that morning is that HR isn't a thing we do, but a way we do business. Andrea was that strategic leader who identified the importance of discussing this concept with those emerging leaders. She wants them to recognize their value, own their perspective, and build strong relationships along the way so that they can lead most effectively through the pivots in their career.

Our passion for encouraging emerging leaders serves us well in building and leading companies. I started early on at Morales Group recognizing that we needed a higher purpose to help us move forward with clarity as a business. Our industry often recruits for jobs in a transactional way, but we decided to build futures while offering employment. We became a cause disguised as a business.

The concept was simple, and we called it ABC (Any job, Better Job, Career). We wanted to provide a path for a person to go from just any job, to a better job, and to eventually have a career. This was our competitive advantage, our WHY was intentionally programmed into this recruiting initiative, and the business took off.

The growth path over the past decade at Morales Group has resulted in annual revenues going from $20M to $145 million and over 200,000 people placed into work. But progress is not always a straight line; there are always moments where things get tough. We've experienced several setbacks as a company—there have been many pivotal moments to lead through. The great recession and pandemic certainly made for difficult storms to weather, but we still managed to put our higher purpose front and center. Some of this we got right, and some of this we got wrong, but we always kept the big picture in mind which was having a cause disguised as a business.

Just like Andrea encourages others to really step in and do the hard work, we knew that type of mindset was needed to make it through. We continue to have a highly engaged team and a healthy culture because we stuck with our big-picture "why." Most importantly, we recognized that **businesses don't grow, people do.** And when you focus on talent as your leading indicator, then you're going to outpace the industry.

As you read these pages, reflect on the pivotal moments in your life and career, and gain insight. Make note of Andrea's emphasis on being courageous, showing up authentically, keeping a big-picture "why," and putting relationships first.

I've watched Andrea build a well-respected leadership consulting practice while developing a community of like-minded leaders who value culture, strategy, and vulnerability. Not to mention Andrea is one of the most authentic people I know, which has led her to becoming not only an amazing leader, but a respected friend. The more companies and people who learn to lead this way, the more people will feel fulfilled and inspired to continue sharing this idea.

— Seth Morales, CEO, Morales Group
1st Year Guest of the *Being [At Work]* Podcast
(see Seth's story beginning on page 37)

INTRODUCTION

HOW & WHY THIS BOOK CAME TO BE

Most of my leadership is set in motion with a gulp and a sigh, not really knowing what I'm doing. Life is a series of pivots, and while I feel cloudy and uncertain much of the time, I can always lean on the anchors in my life—my values, my network, and most importantly, the relationships that lift me up and encourage the best of me. I can choose to step into and stay in the hard stuff.

I am better for leading through the pivots with intentionality, support, and courage. It is the choices we make in the moment that bring meaning to the pivot, but in the chaos of transition and uncertainty, it's hard to know what to do. And in the confusion, I have chosen to bail or chosen the easier path, and I missed out on valuable growth and opportunity in the process.

My career (just like my life) is a journey of twists of turns, full of wise and helpful leaders, challenging leaders, pivots that brought me joy, and pivots doused in pain. If I had only known earlier in my career the value of being anchored in a bigger picture perspective. If I had only known to lean in hard to the people around me. If I had only known the value of staying in the tough moments.

That is why I wrote this book. The pivot is hard and confusing, and yet there are choices in the moment that make it much easier and much more valuable. The purpose of this book is to simplify those choices into three leadership themes, to empower you to lead through the pivots of your life with greater clarity and confidence.

As I grow and mature as a person and a leader (because you cannot separate the two), I am learning to embrace the pivot in all aspects of my life: wife, mom, stepmom, business leader, friend, daughter, sibling, colleague, community leader, board member, neighbor...

Wherever I go, there I am, and my leadership goes with me. My power is in the moment. I am working to respond from a bigger picture perspective and leverage the relationships around me because those are the things that keep me in the game.

My personal ups and downs and all of the pivots along the way have made me who I am—working with leaders all over the world right out of college, leadership learnings through my divorce, being a single mom, beginning new relationships and then ending those relationships, struggling with board leadership, learning how to use my strengths and manage my weaknesses, struggling to influence up, struggling with family relationships, getting married again, becoming a stepmom, leading the enterprise—all of these experiences have strengthened me as a leader and have brought a relatability and connectedness to the work that I do, so I honor each of them.

This book is an exercise in connecting the dots between these personal experiences and the stories I've heard as the host of the leadership podcast, *Being [at Work]*. By looking at the patterns from the stories we've captured and taking the time to reflect on their meaning, there is much to be learned, just as there is much to be learned in the hundreds of stories we have collected since the show launched in July 2019, and each conversation with our guests (executive leaders) begins the same way:

"Tell me about a *pivot*al moment in your career - a situation that taught you a lot about yourself as a leader."

There is greatness in the pivot—growth, challenge, beauty, darkness, and light—all of it. Each story is a valuable leadership lesson and these lessons learned are the crux of the *Being [at Work]* podcast. Since the show's launch, we have uncovered the stories of over 150 executives from unique backgrounds, industries, markets, and types of organizations. Each episode includes an important leadership lesson with unique messages and yet, upon reflection, there are clear themes that emerge. Those themes are worth exploring as they come from the rich stories of executives leading through the challenges we can all relate to (but that are often not shared).

My hope is that in reflecting on the themes that emerged and reading these stories from the first year of the show, you will not shy away from the pivots or the confusion that comes with them, but instead lead through them with greater confidence and clarity.

"**Leading through** the pivots" is the key, and let's be clear on leadership: it is not a position or title—your leadership is in your behavior; it is the influence of the collective choices you make every single day, and we all have the same opportunity to lead—while the context is different for all of us, the opportunity is not unique to anyone. Regardless of whether you are just starting your career, leading as an individual contributor in a large organization, leading a non-profit committee, leading a team of people, leading a board, leading people you do not directly manage, leading your family, leading a new project or venture—YOU are a leader and opportunities for leadership are all around.

I am grateful you have chosen to learn with me. The themes from the *Being [at Work]* stories will provide confidence to lean into the challenges and use them as opportunities for growth. I wish you the courage to pivot with grace and uncover the opportunities for you as you reflect on the stories and the questions presented in this book. With a gulp and a sigh…

THREE THEMES – AN OVERVIEW AND PERSPECTIVE

Leadership is hard. Leading through pivots is hard. It was hard 100 years ago, it's hard now, and it will continue to be hard. As a leader, you are moving someone or something in a new direction, so of course, there will be tension in different shapes and sizes. The best leaders use the tension and the hard situations to grow and get better.

When my daughter Mayson was 8 years old, she participated in a multi-week theatre program to learn basic performance skills. At the beginning of the program, each participant was given a poem to rehearse and practice throughout the program and ultimately, the kids performed their performance at the program's conclusion in front of friends and family.

Mayson was given the Shel Silverstein poem, "Ourchestra" in which she becomes the orchestra: she beat her belly as if it were a drum, played her nose as a horn, etc. It was incredibly cute and engaging, and she practiced continually with so much animation and enthusiasm. It was fun to watch this budding performer; I could not wait to see her on stage.

When performance day arrived, I showed up with my little video recorder and a ton of excitement to cheer Mayson on. On the drive to the theater, she practiced over and over, and did not miss a beat. She had it down and was ready to go.

There was an excitement in the air as the kids began to perform that day. The teacher lined them up on the side of the stage, and as I watched Mayson waiting for her turn, I noticed that her little knees were trembling.

"Oh shoot," I thought. *"I didn't think she'd get nervous."*

When her time came, she stepped onto the make-shift stage and faced the crowd. Her face was ghostly white with red splotches and her hands and knees were trembling. She stood there in complete silence looking at the audience for what felt like an eternity. I wanted to help her – I felt so helpless sitting there in the audience watching her struggle. I put my video camera down and fully expected her to run off the stage and dig her head into my hip sobbing, but that is not what she did. Suddenly, she began to recite the poem. She moved stage left and beat her belly as if it were her drum, and then she moved stage right and played her nose as a horn, all the while reciting each word without missing anything, and she trembled through it all.

I thought of the many times I had run off the stage. When the going got too tough, I would cut and run. But she had not done that. She stayed up there, working her way through it, line by line, trembling throughout, and the audience responded with a standing ovation.

But here's the thing: none of us were clapping because it was a good performance. We were clapping because we'd just witnessed courage. She was visibly petrified, and she did it anyway.

8-year-old Mayson Moore who stayed on the stage (even though she was terrified).

While the scene looks a bit different for an adult leader, many of the same elements apply: practice opportunities, new challenges, the choice to lean into the challenge or not, and how we lead through the difficulties we face. When we step back to reflect on how we showed up in the challenge (or how we fled the scene), we learn a lot about ourselves.

This was the primary reason we launched *Being [at Work.]*. We wanted to hear the tough stories that reflect our humanness at work, how leaders responded in the pivot, and what they most learned about themselves when they reflect on the moments that challenged them the most. I had not expected for the same themes to emerge repeatedly across the stories, but I did know that each story would involve some sort of a challenge.

There is an exercise in a leadership program we facilitate (The Leadership Challenge®) in which we ask leaders to describe a "personal leadership best": a time when they were at their best as a leader. It is an exercise I have been fortunate to facilitate with leaders all over the world for 20 years, and there is something interesting about the outcome: every single personal best I've heard involves a challenge. It's not that *most* of the personal bests involve a challenge; literally, every time I have facilitated the exercise, I ask for participants to raise their hand if their personal best involves a challenge and never once has anyone not raised their hand.

What does that mean? We are up for the challenge. The situations that challenge us the most provide the greatest opportunity for leadership and ultimately, for growth. Think about your own personal best. No doubt it involves a challenge, because ultimately those are the situations we end up (maybe not right away, but at some point) appreciating the most.

This concept is an easy one to grasp for those who like a good physical challenge.

My husband Robert and I have both participated in marathons, half-marathons, triathlons, obstacle races, and other physical challenges, so we were excited to take on our first fourteener a few years ago. Simply put, a "fourteener" is any mountain that exceeds an elevation of 14,000 feet above sea level – it is equivalent to 4,267.2 meters, 2.6 miles, 46.6

football fields, nine and a half Empire State buildings – in other words, it's a long way up.

We did some research and chose Mt. Evans just outside of Denver as we thought it would be more middle-of-the-road in terms of challenge. We set out early one beautiful August morning with some water and trail mix. Based on our research and planning, we expected that it would take about six hours round trip, and that we would be back to the base of the mountain early afternoon.

But that is not what happened.

We somehow misjudged the route and ended up on dangerous terrain multiple times – it was incredibly challenging. As altitude sickness started to set in and a storm approached, we began to pass others who had been to the summit. They encouraged us to turn back. We deliberated and decided to go for it, pushing ahead.

At one point, for over an hour, we climbed, literally crawling on all fours from rock to rock. At another point, I was basically scaling the mountain with my back against the mountain, so I could see straight down. I was terrified. With tears in my eyes, I said a prayer and asked Robert for help.

He shouted, "move your hips," so there I was on the mountain, shimmying, wondering why in the world he was encouraging me to do that. Because of the altitude, he was a bit delirious and had intended to encourage me to *turn* my hips (not move them), as he wanted me to turn and face the mountain. We continue to get a good laugh from that part of the story to this day.

Finally, after eight hours of climbing, pushing ourselves, and encouraging each other, we arrived on the top of the mountain. We were fortunate (and annoyed) to see a parking lot and many visitors at the summit, but grateful to catch a ride down the mountain given that it was getting late in the day.

That was the most physically, mentally, and emotionally challenging experience I have engaged in, AND it is one of my all-time favorite days. We are built to rise to the challenge, and not only does the challenge give us an opportunity to lead, it is invigorating.

Don't let this picture fool you. Moments before this was taken, we were both on the ground, after we collapsed from our tremendous climb.

In hindsight, the challenges that most push us have the greatest opportunity of becoming our personal bests and teaching us the most about ourselves. Knowing that gives us the ability to use "hindsight in advance." Those insurmountable obstacles we thought we would never get through (for me, the hour of literally climbing on all fours) now seems doable. I know that there will be more seemingly insurmountable obstacles in my future and, just as hindsight has proven that I have always been able to work through them, "hindsight in advance" gives me the confidence to stay in the tough moment knowing I will be better for it.

My first role out of graduate school was a Human Resources Assistant for a large, global electronics distributor. The company was headquartered in London, and I worked out of a large division of the company in Chicago. I came into the role wide-eyed, with a ton of enthusiasm, wanting desperately to make an impact.

I quickly became disillusioned by the chasm between what I thought it would be like to work in human resources and the reality. In graduate school, I had learned that the human resources team was the heart of an organization, ensuring that the organization had the right talent, processes, and capability to move the business forward. I supported our sales and marketing function and noticed other HR managers telling leaders what to do and not do. The HR managers got fired up and excited about employee relations issues and people doing things "wrong," and I quickly realized that many of the employee relations issues we were working through could be avoided if we developed stronger leaders.

Rather than coach leaders and equip them to lead through the situation, the HR managers would either do it for them, or tell the leaders what to do. I saw this unfold over and over, and eventually realized that it was a reactive path to nowhere. Since that time, I have committed myself to the proactive development of leaders—equipping leaders to *actually lead.*

18 months into my tenure with the organization, a new HR leader joined the organization. He was progressive and modeled a proactive HR philosophy, similar to what I had learned in graduate school. He recognized the potential within the organization and quickly got to work changing the function and creating a shared vision of HR as a business partner. We worked together to create the first function dedicated to centralized learning and development. At the time, I didn't realize how pivotal this experience would be, but as it unfolded, he asked me to lead the charge on a new team focused on building leadership capability and centralizing learning across our North American businesses.

Developing and equipping leaders has been my passion ever since. I have been fortunate to work with and learn from leaders all over the world and consider myself a curator of great leadership stories. I listen, learn, apply, and share over and over in my work as a facilitator and coach, and the truth is, I am doubtful and insecure through it all. I call at least 10 do-overs every day; I lash out when I shouldn't; I am selfish with my own needs; I don't listen because of my own agenda or fear; I stumble through my words; I cry AND AT THE SAME TIME I believe in and trust life, so I keep going with all of that because I am growing through it all.

Being [at Work] follows the same formula—it has become an important platform to collect leadership stories—both for me as an individual, and for our organization. When we first launched the show, I hadn't planned on writing a book about it. The idea emerged when I reflected on the first year and the details of each story. In preparation for a 1-year anniversary episode, I reviewed the notes I had kept throughout the year and saw the similar patterns across the stories.

Prior to recording each episode, I talk with the guest about the format and ask the big question: "Can you please tell me about a pivotal moment in your career that taught you a lot about yourself and your leadership?"

There is a precious moment when I see or hear the guest remembering and reflecting on the joy and/or the pain of the situation. "Oh, yeah," they'll say, "there was this one time when..." and they're off to the races.

Often guests will say "I don't know if I should talk about that," and immediately I encourage, "if you are feeling some tension, then that is MOST DEFINITELY the story you need to tell."

Through each of the episodes, there have been many tears, and a lot of laughter. It's been intense and awkward and delightful and everything in between. There is something magical about recalling these stories and creating a space for them. We all have those kinds of moments of big, big learning and, what I've noticed is how invigorating it is to reflect on and share those stories. The stories are a reminder that **your humanity is showing just like everyone else's.**

It is interesting how readily these leaders open up and share their stories with so much vulnerability and passion. Following each of the recordings, guests regularly share how much they enjoyed the process and the reflection opportunity. Perhaps we should all do that more often?

Throughout the rest of this book, we will explore effective leadership in the challenging moments. What has driven successful leaders to stay on the stage and maximize the power in the pivot? In reflecting on your own personal best or a pivotal moment, what do you think those themes are? What keeps you going during a challenge? Why did Mayson stay on the stage? Why did Robert and I push on to the summit with a storm on the horizon? As I reflect on these personal examples and the stories collected during the first year of *Being [at Work]*, these are the leadership practices to take you from chaos to clarity:

1. **Going bigger-picture**
2. **Focusing on the relationships**
3. **Stepping into and staying in the hard stuff**

These three leadership behaviors bring power to the pivot. They are evidence-based. They showed up in the stories of over 50 tenured executives when asked to talk about a pivotal moment that taught them something about themselves and their leadership.

Certainly, there is a connectivity and a supportive relationship amongst them as a triad, but it is also helpful to look at each of them individually. There are many important leadership behaviors within each of these themes that we can all leverage every single day in all aspects of our lives. Remember: wherever you go, there you are, and wherever you are, there is an opportunity for leadership.

Pivotal moments are all around us. They can be as insignificant as a frustration in the grocery store line or trying to get your kids out the door, or as big as not getting the promotion or a challenging relationship with your boss or colleague. Regardless of their size or significance, we can always, in every single situation, go big picture, focus on the relationships, and step into and stay in the hard stuff. Each of these actions is completely within our control.

As I reflect on our fourteener experience, those themes are apparent and, ultimately, they are the drivers that kept us heading towards the summit. We had a goal: our plan was to complete a fourteener, to hike to over 14,000 feet. We wanted to accomplish that goal, so when it got tough, we reminded ourselves of that, and we leveraged each other for encouragement and support along the way.

There was a portion of the mountain that was all rock – *big* rocks – we were on our all fours for over an hour climbing from rock to rock. The only way to get through it was one rock at a time. It represents the hard stuff that we had to step into – it was the only way we were going to accomplish our goal.

Finally, and most importantly, I could not have done it without Robert, and I honestly do not think Robert could have done it without me. We supported and encouraged each other throughout it and needed each other to keep us going. The relationship was mission-critical; struggling together, laughing together, supporting each other, and going through the challenge as a team helped us to accomplish our goal.

Another interesting dynamic about this story is that when we first set out that morning, we were going to do the entire hike in silence – a "silent fourteener" we had planned. We stuck to that plan for about an hour – it was awkward passing other hikers who spoke to us and eventually it got challenging and we wanted to talk to support each other. We needed to talk to get through it.

Do you notice the connection between the themes? They are all supportive of each other and the sequence is also important. The big picture gives you something to anchor to and to strive for. It is your "why." The people involved and the relationships drive commitment and give you courage to step into and lead through the challenge. Between the base of the mountain and the summit (our big-picture goal), there was a lot of work to be done and, one step at a time, we got there. But we could not have done it without each other.

These three themes—going big picture, focusing on the relationships, and stepping into and staying in the hard stuff— are the power in the PIVOT.

There will always be pivotal moments and *the choices we make in relation to the challenges* define our leadership. Choose to go big picture, focus on the relationships, and step into and stay in the hard stuff. Over the next few chapters, we will explore each in detail and see how they played out in the stories we heard during the first year of our show.

Please note that at the end of each chapter, I have included reflection questions to support YOU, as you lead through the inevitable pivots in your life. I encourage you to take time to reflect on these questions and explore the answers that emerge. Here's to leading through the pivots with much grace and intentionality.

THEME 1: GO BIG PICTURE

"We don't see the world as it is; we see it as we are."

— ANAÏS NIN

1

POWERING UP TO GO BIG
PICTURE

*W*e are all walking around as the lead characters in our own crazy stories.

Whether you realize it or not, you are creating it all as you go, based on how you think about it. That is the most empowering aspect of life because, when you get that, you realize just how powerful you are. You hold the key in your mind, which is why the FIRST and most important principle in leading through any pivot is going bigger-picture. You've got to get your ego (and others' expectations) out of the way and anchor to something bigger. In other words, there is value in developing the discipline of using your thoughts to get out of the muck of what is and image the possibilities of what could be.

Many years ago, I set a goal to run my first half-marathon (13.1 miles), so I joined a running group through the local YMCA to prepare for the race. Each week, we met as a group and increased our mileage leading up to the half-marathon we were all training for. There were about 20 people in the group, and at the beginning of the program, our coach took time to talk with us about the basics of running and asked each of us to set and share our specific goal for the program/race. My goal was to run the entire half-marathon—I didn't have a specific time goal

—I just wanted to complete it. I remember in the moment we were sharing our goals, I added a second goal: I wanted to meet new people as there were some interesting people in the group.

As I reflect on the experience now, it is clear that our goals for the program shaped our participation in the program. I quickly befriended two other women who had similar goals and ran at a similar pace. During one of our long runs, our coach ran alongside us for a bit and was giving us a bit of a hard time about talking during the run. He laughed and said, "Andrea, if you used all of the energy it takes for you to talk to others and cheer them on, you could run a lot faster." Most definitely, he was right, but when I filter my choice to talk and encourage while running through my goals, I was doing exactly what I needed to do to accomplish them. If I had not set those goals, I may have sped up and missed out on an opportunity to make new friends.

My goals in this story represent the bigger picture. Because my goal was to run without walking and meet new people, I had a foundation from which to make choices on how to show up in the process. That is the value in having a bigger picture to leverage.

Think of the bigger picture as the foundation, or your anchor—the why behind your choices. As you'll read in the stories that follow, the foundation can show up in many different forms: mission, vision, goals, affirmations, values, etc. It doesn't matter as much WHAT it is that is providing the foundation. The important thing is having a foundation from which to make choices. It's the difference between living life by default and reacting to everything that's coming at you, and living life BY DESIGN.

That is why I named this first theme "go big-picture." I toyed with other ways in which to summarize the theme and considered including "vision" in the name to denote the value in having a clear direction or path. I chose not to do that because in my experience, people often get hung up on the word vision; it is intimidating for many. When thinking about a vision, leaders often put pressure on themselves to create a beautifully crafted statement, but there is an important distinction in this first theme: having a vision is not the theme that showed up in our guests' stories. The theme that emerged is the practice of going big-picture amidst challenge. In other words, coming up from the muck of "what is" to focus more broadly.

The value here is broader than a future-focus: it's a combination of a strong foundation and the ability to see out beyond obstacles.

There are two practical actions that support this value—the discipline in "coming up from the muck" and the intentionality in "focusing more broadly" regardless of what the broader focus is. This gets us unstuck and out of obstacle-thinking. This practice of coming up and going big-picture frees us up to imagine new possibilities and to align our actions to something important to us.

Here are two simple examples:

HRD Vision and Values

I joined HRD – A Leadership Development Company in 2017 as the President of the organization. Throughout my first two years with the organization, we experienced significant growth, including our best year in the history of the organization in 2019. We began and experienced the first two months of 2020 with a lot of optimism and aggressive growth targets, with a focus on growing current accounts and adding new ones. None of us imagined that we would be leading through a pandemic.

Throughout 2020, we led through the global pandemic and a shifting market. Revenue was down, opportunities disappeared, and we had to adapt and flex as a team, as most organizations did, and we emerged better for it. We relied on our shared vision and our values throughout (both bigger-picture support).

Our long-term vision at the time was to be acquired, so during tough conversations in which we disagreed on our course of action, we would often ask, "When we filter this situation through our goal of being acquired, what makes sense?"

Similarly, our core values are anchors that we created as a team, so we ask ourselves in a critical moment or a disagreement, "What would our values do right now?" "What would growth, connection, and service do right now?" As Roy Disney (the oldest brother of Walt Disney) said, "It's not hard to make decisions when you know what your values are."

A new client opportunity emerged during the pandemic. It was an exciting global opportunity which required us to stretch. At one point in the sales process, because it was a tough assignment, I almost bowed out and told them that we were not the right partner for them. However, in stepping back and filtering the challenge through our vision and values, it became clear that a partnership would be of great value to both of us. When I removed myself from the muck of the tough situation and reflected more broadly through the lens of our values and vision, I had the motivation necessary to move forward with confidence.

While the bigger-picture was certainly helpful in leading through the pandemic, its importance was established by taking the time to engage the entire team in building this foundation. It was a foundation that preceded my leadership, so it was important for me to take that into account. I was approached by HRD's founders in early 2017 about leading the organization which had been established in 1996. It was a profitable business with deep expertise and legacy clients, so there was much potential for growth, and yet the founders were nearing retirement and looking to pass the baton to someone new, to bring new energy and perspective to the business. It was an ideal opportunity for me, having worked for many years at a competitor consulting firm and also having spent many years in the shoes of our ideal customer, leading talent and HR functions within mid- and large-scale organizations. Just prior to my transition, I connected with an old JFK quote that I used as influence in the leadership role at HRD to balance the rich history and move the organization into the future:

"Hold fast to the best of the past and move fast to the best of the future."

— JOHN F. KENNEDY

Within two months of joining the organization, observing team members, the dynamics in the business, and collecting feedback from customers, together (founders, owners, all team members, and myself) we went through a strategic planning process to identify our vision, values, and focus areas. It was a process that took some time and tough conversations, but a two-page strategic plan outlining our focus emerged. We co-created a shared vision that we reviewed and updated each month and continue to do so each year. Through challenging conversations or lack of focus, it has provided direction and a sense of confidence in where we are headed as a team.

Parenting Vision and Values

My oldest daughter, Mayson (who stayed on the stage), is now studying at Indiana University (go Hoosiers!). Because we are so closely connected, I expected that her transition to college (and out of our home) would be more challenging for me. And it has, but not in the way I expected.

Mayson experienced a traumatic event a couple of months before leaving for college. She took the trauma with her, so there have been many tearful Facetimes and phone calls. I have learned through this experience that she has her own path, and I cannot "fix" or solve her problems. My vision for our relationship is that I am a soft place for her to fall in times of challenge. There is a bigger picture at play. When I get messages expressing anxiety or fear, I rely on the bigger picture: she is growing through it all and the challenges are part of the process. I am her soft place to fall; that is my role. So I repeat "You are ok; this is challenging moment; I am here for you," and often, I just sit with her in silence (which is excruciatingly hard for me). That broader perspective and the vision for my role keeps me grounded in the moment and helps me to respond thoughtfully and helpfully.

WHY THIS THEME OF BIG-PICTURE FIRST?

This is the first theme for the reasons highlighted in both the HRD and parenting examples. **Going bigger-picture gets us out of the muck of what is and allows us to get beyond obstacle thinking.** It allows us to see clearly amidst the chaos. This concept applies both personally and organizationally. Across year one of *Being [at Work]*, there were many pivotal moments that centered around the impact of taking the time to build the organization's foundation, and in many of the examples, these leaders highlighted how the process started with their own personal reflection.

Because you are a leader, you cannot separate your leadership growth from your growth as a human being. Since you are always evolving as a human being, your leadership growth is constant. The key is to recognize what you are learning along the way. Grace naturally flows from this attitude. Knowing that we are works in progress helps us to give ourselves grace in moments of challenge. We are so hard on ourselves, and take ourselves way too seriously (yes, this is the kettle calling the pot black 😊). As my family can attest, I can turn any situation into a coaching moment, so it is important to balance the seriousness of learning with the levity of grace and light. We can grow without heaviness if we approach it with balance, another big-picture perspective.

In their best-selling book, *The Leadership Challenge*, authors Jim Kouzes & Barry Posner outline The Five Practices of Exemplary Leadership®. Not surprisingly, the outcomes of the first two practices within this model are the foundation that showed up in our first theme, go big-picture (both the coming up from the muck and the ability to focus on the future). The first two practices are modeling the way and inspiring a shared vision. This is affirming, as The Five Practices of Exemplary Leadership® come from over 40 years of research and Kouzes and Posner asking the question, "When leaders are at their best, what are they doing?"

I was fortunate to sit down with Jim Kouzes in **Episode 018, The Story Behind *The Leadership Challenge* Journey.**

Jim Kouzes: I feel very blessed and grateful that early in my career I was able to find a partner with whom I could work. We have complementary strengths. Barry enjoys doing the research, and I really like the practical side. We've both, over time writing so much together, been able to blend those two together in a way that feels like one singular voice.

Early on we realized that we write about values, we write about people having to have some principles that guide them along their path, and we decided that we needed to do that for ourselves. We needed to ask ourselves, "What are the fundamental principles for which we stand that are integrated throughout our work, that inform our work, both the practical side and then the research and academic side?" and the first one of those is collaboration.

One of the most memorable lessons I ever learned from the people we interviewed was Don Bennett during the first edition. I asked Don to share the most important lesson he learned in climbing Mount Rainier (fourteen thousand four hundred ten feet on one leg and two poles). And he said, "You can't do it alone," so collaboration has been a very important part of our work. We share everything 50/50. Essentially, we work together in our writing and in the training and the work that we do in consulting and coaching as equal partners. That is number one, and it infuses our work because we have learned that you can't do it alone.

Jim and Barry's partnership for over 40 year is a testament to the foundation of shared values—their big picture focus. During our conversation, I asked him how their values have supported them in challenging times.

Jim: I can tell you that whenever you are working together for any length of time or in any kind of close relationship,

9

there's always disagreements. There is always potentially some tension that might be around failure to meet a deadline or deadlines approaching and the other person has completed their work, for example, if Barry has done his, or vice versa, or we happen to disagree about a particular key message or how it's phrased. We are always doing that, and we've been fortunate to be able to sit down and talk through them.

COACHING QUESTIONS

- What does "going big-picture" mean to you?
- What strategy(s) will you try on to get out of the muck and go big-picture to imagine the possibilities?

2

STARTING WITH YOU

*W*hat are you anchored to?

This question is at the core of powering up to go big-picture, and it is the key to staying grounded in the inevitable pivots. As Kenny Rogers says, "You've got to stand for something, or you'll fall for anything."

You can apply this question to any situation or relationship in your life and it will ALWAYS bring you back to your foundation. Call the anchor what you want—values, vision, mission, goal, direction—the purpose is the same: to provide a calm focus and remind you why you are doing what you are doing.

During my experience with the running group, I was anchored to the fact that I wanted to finish the half-marathon I was signed up for and make friends in the process. I did both. If I had set a specific time goal, my participation in the group would have looked a bit different.

As I reflect more deeply on the running group experience, I can also see how my core values were reflected in the goals I set. Connection is a core value for me—I get energy from meeting and connecting with people. My core values are an important anchor in my life and as I intentionally integrate them into my day-to-day activities, I lead with authenticity and consistency.

What are your core values? Have you ever gone through a process or taken the time to identify and name them?

During the conversation with Jim Kouzes, he referenced that he and Barry Posner had taken leaders through the exercise of facilitating their core values because of the strength in the foundation of core values.

During my conversation with **Trey Willis (Episode 001: Clarifying Your Personal Values),** the Chief Technology Officer at CTSI-Global, he talked about his pivotal moment in going through the process of clarifying his personal values and getting feedback from others.

> **Trey:** *I'm a football player, a lifelong athlete, and have been coached all my life, and some of the things that come along with athletics are things like being tough and persevering and not letting your weakness show. For many years, I found success with those characteristics.*
>
> *Several years ago, I attended a leadership workshop. I was a young, aspiring leader and was very focused on getting the job done. I thought that's how we needed to do everything all the time. During the workshop, we were led through a process to clarify our personal values to be more authentic. I learned that to garner leadership credibility, I needed to be as clear and consistent as possible in my everyday communication and everyday behaviors as a leader so that the folks around me would understand who I am as a leader and what the guiding principles are for how I operate.*

Trey went on to describe the exercise as "life changing," because he realized that he was a different person at home than he was at the office. At home and in his personal life, he led with much more humor, but he didn't bring that into his leadership role at work. He learned that wherever he goes, there he is, and he takes his values with him. By acting on them in all aspects of his life, they become a source of consistency and strength wherever he is.

> *Trey: I asked myself "Is this who I really am or who I want to be?" I took the five values I came up with through the exercise and typed it up and sent it out to several of my closest friends and family and asked them for feedback. I asked them to share the values they saw in me, and they validated the list, and I felt really at peace with that. I said to myself, "This is really who you are," and I hit the "go" button. I don't need to be Jekyll and Hyde. I told myself, "Just be the guy. People seem OK with that guy, and so Trey, you need to be OK with that guy."*

It becomes easier to make decisions when you know what your values are, because there's something to anchor your choices to. It doesn't even matter what "it" is—once you've identified your core values, you can filter any situation through them.

For many years, I worked with a sales leader who connected with people quickly through his humor and quick wit—it broke the ice and set the tone, and people loved him because of it. So for quite some time, I worked to "be funnier." I even sought counsel from a comedian friend to help me integrate more humor into my interactions, but the harder I worked to be funnier, the less funny I was.

One day, my comedian friend said to me in passing, "You are a fun, positive person; stop trying to be funny, and be that."

My colleague's humor worked so well for him because it was authentic to who he is. We lead from the essence of who we are as people. My trying to be funny came off as forced, but positivity, as my comedian friend reminded me, is natural to who I am, so when I lead with that, it feels very real. Positivity is a core value of mine, and in any situation, I can ask, "what would positivity do?" and rest assured that a natural response will follow.

As Trey's story highlights, our core values provide a strong foundation from which to lead with consistency. They serve as a constant support system if we have the courage to define and act upon them.

J.J. Barnes (Episode 036: Getting My Mojo Back) is the chief marketing officer at enVista, a leading global software solutions and consulting services firm. J.J.'s commitment to her core values is apparent throughout her career, and yet a few years ago, she found herself in doubt. Fortunately, she knows what she is anchored to. Through the ups and downs, her values have remained constant.

> *JJ: I'm sitting here in middle age and it kind of all makes sense now. But boy, through all the chapters and changes, it didn't make sense at all, and I really didn't know what I wanted to be when I grew up. I was an overachiever, a dancer, someone that loved to read, and I showed up completely underprepared in terms of what I wanted to do from a professional standpoint. The common denominator that got me through to today are the themes of connection, hard work, curiosity and faith – those four pieces all woven together.*

I appreciate how J.J. describes her values as "pieces all woven together." It is the combination of her values that proved to be the common denominator, as the values are always there. As I write these words, I'm cognizant of the green post-it-note on my laptop where my core values are written: positivity, integrity, service, and connection. They are my anchors. There are many times when my ego or personality kicks in, so this post-it note reminder is always there bringing me back to actions that honor who I am at my core. I can always ask, "What would my core values do in this situation?" It's encouraging to know I can always rely on them in this way.

Conversely, when I feel "off" or something doesn't sit well, I can go to my values. Most of the time in these situations, I failed to demonstrate a value.

Many months ago, I delivered bad news to a team member via text message. I was on a family camping trip, and rather than taking the time to call him or wait until I returned, I took the easy route, a route that was not aligned with my values.

Fortunately, because of the relationship I have with this team member, he called me out on it, and we were able to talk through it. Had I taken the time to filter the situation through my values, I would have called him rather than texting him the update.

So, what are you anchored to? Can you list your core values? Can you rattle them off in the middle of a challenging situation to provide direction? Take some time to reflect on your own non-negotiables, your foundation, so that you have a safe place to fall.

Each Sunday, I take time to plan for the week—it is a rhythm that works well for me and has become a part of my routine. I take time to review my long-term vision, short-term goals, and I note what I am most thankful for.

Because I lead a professional services business, much of my focus and my gratitude revolves around new opportunities and driving new business. Recently, when I received an email from a prospective client to whom we had been talking for months, saying that they were not ready to engage in the work we had proposed, my initial reaction was disappointment. But when I filtered the situation through my values, they quickly brought me back to a growth mindset and a faith in what is and will be.

Moments like these happen throughout each of our days, as life is full of little disappointments. We always have 100% control over our response in these situations, but we often get hooked by the disappointment and can easily spiral into a web of negativity—blaming, rationalizing, defending—all of which are completely wasted energy. Leaders RESPOND rather than react, so it is helpful to prepare ourselves to respond. It is like baseball players engaging in batting practice: they are preparing themselves for the game. When leaders take time to reflect on their bigger picture values and vision, they equip themselves to respond in a more helpful way in the moment.

In the situation with the prospective client, there is so much more behind the scenes that I am not aware of and I don't control any of that. Trying to control it would be futile, so instead I chose to respond to the email with faith, integrity, acceptance and trust that we will partner with them when the time is right. That is taking charge of my life. I trust that the focus and attention we're giving to new business development will play out just as it should. I can't control this particular situation, but I can control how I show up and respond from my values.

Eleanor Roosevelt once said, "In the long run, we shape our lives, and we shape ourselves. The process never ends until we die. And the choices we make are ultimately our own responsibility."

Everything is always what we choose to make of it. *Everything*. Knowing and getting this ensures that we are much more thoughtful about how we respond to and talk about challenges. **Terry Holloway, Senior Vice President and Chief People Officer at Strada Education Network (Episode 009: Battling Selfish Thoughts)** shared a story that represents this well.

> *Terry Holloway: Maybe you are at that point in your career as a leader or as an individual contributor where things should be happening for you. You may be thinking: I've got enough tenure now; I've been here long enough. Why am I not getting that promotion or why am I not seeing things happen for me? I'm not getting good projects. I'm being left out of the information loop. Well, sometimes those things are out of your control. If you have that good base of confidence that you do good work and seek others' opinions and remain humble through it, that can lead you through difficult challenges.*
>
> *I worked for an organization during a significant economic downturn, and I was at a point where I really believed that I should have that next-level promotion. I felt like, based on what I was hearing, that I should have had a bigger role by*

then. But it wasn't about me. It was about this company finding its footing to drive forward and grow in the wake of a bad economy. I was fortunate during that time and throughout my career to have great mentors. I was and am very blessed in my career to have great people to share the bigger picture and remind me to have patience and remind me that the organization didn't feel any less about me. I needed to continue to do great work and find new ways to get involved, to stretch laterally. Good lateral opportunities are immeasurably important to your career. Broaden your skills and do things that you may even find that you enjoy even more than the job that you thought you wanted to capstone your career. Through that challenging time, I learned a lot. It wasn't about me getting what I wanted – it was about me continuing to grow and continuing to learn and bring people in.

As Terry's example highlights, going big-picture starts with you and your attitude. There's an important message of humility in his message and trusting that life is giving you what you need. I can relate to his sentiment of believing I should get that promotion and more opportunity. After a few years working at a consulting organization and having tremendous success, I became greedy and wanted more. I remember my leader at the time cautioning me about "getting too big for my britches," and it really bugged me at the time. Now I get it, and I appreciate the message. My wanting something else took my eyes off of the growth and opportunity where I was.

With a growth mindset, leaders are in a better position to stay open to the opportunities and recognize that they are growing through it all. **Scott Miller, President at Bowman Construction (Episode 024: Nothing Great Happens Without Adversity)** shared a story that highlights this.

Scott: I had been at a previous organization for about 10 years, and we had just had our best year ever. The owners called me in and said, "Hey, Scott, we've been really happy with where things have been, but we think we need to go in a different direction at this point in time." I was crushed and could feel anger and all the different emotions that come up —I had been a part of helping to build something amazing. It taught me that no matter what, I'm not the one in control. From my perspective, there are always unique opportunities ahead of you, even when something seemingly bad takes place. It led me to be a part of the economic development team in Indianapolis and to travel the world, and I never would have done that had I continued in that role. Now, as difficult or bad things pop up, I know there is a plan out there that's bigger than what we know. You have to try to find the opportunity in whatever you're going through.

Call it what you want—vision, mission, values, the bigger picture—the goal is the same: to anchor yourself to something broader than the challenge.

When I first joined HRD, I struggled to build a relationship with one of the company's owners—his leadership style was hands-off, but he expected a high level of growth. The lack of connection was hard for me, as I was used to working collaboratively and supportively with leaders.

Rather than working to build a relationship, I focused on getting results to make him happy. The first time he challenged me on something, I went into victim mode, feeling that he was the problem for not supporting me. Instead of appropriately leading my relationship with him, I let my ego lead, and the first time it was bruised, the dysfunction arose quickly.

Across the first year of *Being [at Work]*, there are several examples about not falling into victim mode. Leaders don't allow themselves to become victims, but instead they use the challenges as opportunities.

Going big-pictures starts with you; it takes awareness of the thoughts and choices that are keeping you from getting what it is you want.

Maia Siprashvilli – Lee (Episode 019: Choosing Family AND Career in a New Environment) has spent her career in government leadership. She moved to the United States in 2013 from her home country of Georgia, where she served as National Deputy Minister of Defense. Her story highlights perseverance through a major life transition, not just on her own, but also with her family. She focuses on influencing challenges by changing her inner world. In other words, she started with herself...

> *Maia: Sometimes it requires suppressing your ego and really looking at a bigger picture and saying, "OK, this is a stepping-stone. You know your potential. You know who you are, and this is where you start from." I had to start life over many times. This was a new environment, new continent, new country, and sometimes I would look at it as a challenge. I would try to be an observer to say, "How is my life going? Remember when you went to NATO headquarters and did this and did that." And then I would just say, "OK, ego, we are here now."*
>
> *What really helped me to keep going was getting out of feeling sorry for myself. That's really what it was. I said, "Enough. This is where I am, and I am going to open up to new opportunities. This is my reality now, so how can I make the best of it?"*

Maia's story is an important reminder that when you shift your perspective about the situation, the situation changes. When you filter the situation through your values, a more helpful solution emerges.

One of my all-time favorite books is *Man's Search for Meaning* by Viktor Frankl. Frankl was an Austrian psychologist who spent many years in a concentration camp during World War II. His book chronicles his experiences and his learning that everything can be taken from a man but the most fundamental human freedom: man's ability to choose his response in any situation. That book was perspective-setting for me—if Frankl could adopt that attitude living in a conception camp, surely I can apply it to the privileged, cushy world I live in.

I felt similarly when talking with **Katara McCarty (Episode 029: Reclaiming and Rewriting Your Story)**. I talked with Katara through tears, listening to her heartfelt story, another incredible example of not falling into victim mode. At birth, Katara was abandoned in the hospital by her mother who was ashamed of birthing a baby with her African American boyfriend. Katara went from the hospital at birth into the foster care system.

> *Katara: That happened to me, but that doesn't have to own me. It doesn't dictate how I show up today. I am rewriting my story, taking ownership of my life, and taking my power back. That's where the power comes from. That's where we square our shoulders. I will never forget when I heard the quote by Marianne Williamson: "Our deepest fear is not that we are inadequate. Our deepest fear is that we are powerful beyond measure. It is our light, not our darkness, that most frightens us. Your playing small does not serve the world. There is nothing enlightened about shrinking so that other people won't feel insecure around you. And as we let our light shine, we unconsciously give other people permission to do the same. And as we are liberated from our own fear, our presence automatically liberates others."*

> *When I heard that quote, it rocked me to my core. I thought, "Oh my gosh, I've created a pattern in my life of shrinking!" Because of life circumstances, because of things that have happened, I have practiced and gotten really good at shrinking, and it wasn't serving me, and it wasn't serving the world. When I decided to square my shoulders and to embrace my light and say yes to my light and to let it start shining, things started taking off for me. That's what I choose to do, is to let my light shine, because then I give other women, other people permission to do the same.*

COACHING
QUESTIONS

- What are you anchored to?
- What strategy(s) will you try on to build your foundation so that you have a bigger picture to go to?

3

LETTING THE BIG-PICTURE PULL YOU

*D*uring a long run recently, I got caught up in the sunshine, the beautiful day, and a feeling of complete connectedness with life. I was on the trail near my home and suddenly, there was a clearing and the sun emerged and I could feel life pulling me forward. I opened my hands in surrender and closed my eyes. I'm not sure where that came from, and it didn't last long, but in that moment, life was pulling me along. I lost all track of time, and even the fact that I was running.

Michael Beckwith, spiritual teacher, and founder of the Agape International Spiritual Center, says that "pain pushes until the vision pulls." That pain, that daily struggle, is life's way of pushing you towards your purpose. Each experience is an important part of the whole. Rather than feeling the pain of my run, for a moment my sole focus was on something much bigger.

When life and/or the still small voice within you is reminding you of your bigger purpose, do you pay attention to it? Do you give it space and explore it?

Jim Morris (Episode 032: Failure is Where You Grow), CEO of the Greater Indianapolis Habitat for Humanity describes this feeling of being pulled by a bigger vision.

> *Jim:* I landed in this space of not knowing exactly what was
> next. I was invited to come into the residential building and
> development industry through sales, so I took it because I
> needed to find work after graduating. I jumped in, and I
> was not somebody who was naturally inclined to be the
> sales guy, but the training actually was incredibly valuable
> around the sales process. It was a great foundation for me,
> and at the same time, I had never been introduced to resi-
> dential building and construction. You definitely didn't
> want me building your house with my lack of skill set, but I
> really grew a passion for helping guide families, particu-
> larly young families, through the process of purchasing
> their first home. There was something in there—the teach-
> ing, training, and guiding them so that they would be
> successful, that there was a seed plant there and that even-
> tually came full circle. That was a vital time for me to learn
> and to understand that this was something I actually had a
> passion for. There was always a yearning that I had inside
> to do something that was more missional based.

Many years ago, when I was working as a consultant at a growing firm, I felt the yearning Jim describes. I regularly thought about and talked with the owners of the firm about a daily leadership message. I was working with leaders all over the country, coaching and facili-tating leadership development and I dreamed of getting more content to them more regularly and consistently, but the idea never came to fruition. It never seemed to fit into the strategy for that business, but fast forward to today, and each day, we publish a Daily Dose of Lead-ership through our *Being [at Work]* podcast. These two-to-three minute leadership nuggets fulfill that yearning that I felt many years ago, wanting to share regular leadership encouragement and inspiration.

Often, the yearning gets ignored or rationalized away, and sometimes it is the ideas that others have about our path that keep us from following our own hearts. **Amy Vaughan (Episode 041: Choosing Success for Yourself, Not the Status Quo)** recalls her pivotal moment as the realization that she had chosen a path for others rather than herself. Prior to her current role as the CEO of Together Digital, Amy worked as an award-winning creative director, creating compelling digital and video content for brands such as Ford, Pringles, Walmart, Fifth, Third Bank and many more. Her writing and perspectives on the industry have also been featured in multiple well-known publications. She's now on a path that is aligned with her strengths and passion, but early in her career, she focused on what would make others proud, rather than what she would be happiest doing.

> *Amy: I fell into that trap pretty early on, as I started college pre-med. I don't even really know what made me choose that major. I thought, well, being a doctor sounds honorable. I think it requires you to be smart. And you get to help people. I think my parents would be proud of that. Unfortunately, I really did not excel at math or biology or chemistry, but I tried.*

It took her several years to tap into her creative and graphic design strengths and into a path that honors her passion. She notes her greatest advice to emerging leaders is to define success for yourself, not the status quo. When I asked her about acknowledging her creative talents, she talked about how marketing found her; the creative strengths she felt as a young age found a place in her career:

> *Amy: It was not something that was championed. My grandfather was an amazing artist. He was an illustrator, and my mom as well; she can paint, she can sew, she can pretty much do anything, and not just the crazy stuff. She is an artist. At a young age, I loved writing poetry and music and drawing, but because neither of them had success in*

pursuing it professionally and both felt very self-conscious and very critical of their own work and of each other's, it was just between the three of us. It's funny to see a history and heritage of family talent that went to the wayside because of that ripple effect.

So, I did realize that I was creative from a young age, but it was just for me. It wasn't for everybody else and it wasn't seen as productive. And that is what I liked about advertising—I could be creative, but I wasn't being creative just for myself. I was helping solve a business's problem or was helping somebody else solve a problem with a product, so I found advertising appealing because of that, because for once I could be creative and get paid and it felt productive.

Sometimes, the bigger picture and the yearning pulls you to start a movement. **Jill Trimmel (Episode 020: On a Mission to Close the Gap in Pay Equality)** is leading an effort to close the gap in pay equality (check it out at: https://www.iwillclosethegap.com). This effort was born from a pivotal moment in her career in which she reflected on her impact. She had been promoted multiple times and often found herself being the only woman at the table in a male-dominated industry. During a conference, she looked around the room at her male colleagues and asked herself, "What have I changed?" She reflected on an issue that was very important to her: pay equality.

Jill: Throughout my career, I had coached women on negotiating their salary and understanding their value, but as I sat there at this big meeting, I thought "Here I am again, the only woman at the table, and what have I really changed?"

When I got home, I started researching. I spent a lot of time looking at different sources on pay equality, hoping to validate that I changed something. I wanted to get rid of that

*feeling, but through the research, I came to believe that I
hadn't changed anything. I learned that the gender pay gap
had remained stagnant the previous two years and that, for
the first time in decades, we had not made any progress at
all. I decided right then that I was going to do something,
that I had to do something, and I just felt compelled to
create change.*

The bigger picture perspective that Jill gained pulled her to do something. When starting his business, Innovatemap, **Mike Reynolds (Episode 048: Lessons on Hustle or Starting a New Business)** also leveraged the feeling of being overwhelmed by the bigger picture. Innovatemap is a product agency, helping companies of all sizes dream, design, and deliver digital products and services to market. Mike is considered a visionary in the digital space, specifically in the areas of product management.

> **Mike:** *The vision is everything. You are going to get your ass
> kicked, and the only thing keeping you getting up is the
> world that you see one year, three year and five years out.
> It's the only thing keeping you going. It isn't just that you
> saw something good. It was your hourly and daily driver
> during very, very rough moments.*

Prior to starting Innovatemap, Mike had always thought if he was going to start a company it would be a software company because that was the business he knew. Instead, he started a service business, which he was less familiar with, because he could not ignore the market opportunity he saw.

> **Mike:** *I had a software idea three times a week, but none of
> them compelled me or I didn't see the full market opportu-
> nity for them, and when I saw the agency opportunity, it
> overwhelmed me.*

YES! The vision does overwhelm--that is how it pulls you, but only if you're paying attention. In the muck of what is, we often get sucked in and keep doing what we're doing, living by default. Pay attention to being inspired by something bigger and allow yourself to imagine the possibilities. Why not?

COACHING QUESTIONS

- What is pulling you?
- What strategy(s) will you try on to let go and allow life to lead you?

4

REINVENTING YOURSELF

*E*ach pivot teaches us something about ourselves. Much of the leadership journey involves leaders discovering who they are and what life and their leadership really means to them. My experience has led me to believe that life is not about finding yourself, it is about creating yourself. **Your leadership journey is about discovering what you are capable of and learning from your challenges to evolve into the person and leader you aspire to be.**

Sit with that for a moment.

In recognizing that, doesn't it take the pressure off? We are always evolving and getting better, so it serves us well to let go of the striving and lean into curiosity.

As I lead leaders through self-awareness exercises, I enjoy doing the exercises with them. Over and over, I check in with myself. I have clarified my personal values hundreds of times, and have shifted how I name them and talk about them over the years and the updated bigger pictures (my updated core values) are helpful with whatever current leadership challenges I am facing.

As the challenges evolve, so does the bigger picture, because I am evolving as life evolves. In this way, there is a symbiotic relationship between me and the challenges I am facing, so naturally, I am reinventing myself and I stay in the current challenge and learn through it.

M.T. Ray's (episode 002: Reinventing Yourself) story highlights the personal evolution through the challenge. M.T. knows that the leadership journey is about discovering who you are and what you are capable of, as her pivotal moment came from being forced to reinvent herself. She is the previous Vice President of Human Resources at Advanced Agrilytics (along with many other organizations) and has seen tremendous success as a talent leader in the technology space—as I reflect on her path, it's clear that her ability to reinvent herself has served her well.

> *M.T.: It was my time. Two years into a role I was very engaged in, the organization decided to move forward with a downsizing due to financial difficulties; I was a critical part of managing the downsizing, and on the last day, I was pulled into an office and told that my role had been impacted, as well, so I also lost my position. It was quite the blow to my ego and my confidence. Totally unexpected, I was surprised by the whole thing. I went home that night thinking, "I'm over 40; I jumped back in and now, I have to figure out what I'm going to do next." I wasn't sure what that was going to be, so I spent some time grieving a bit.*

> *I was lucky enough to be given some outplacement help, so I was able to work with a career coach to get my resume back together and be the confidence booster to get me out there and take some risks to network and meet some people. This was in 2009, so the economy was not great. Human Resources positions, as I was looking for, were not roles that were being filled. Companies didn't have budget to add that overhead, so it was a lot more challenging, so I had to step back and look at: what did I want to do? What did I*

need to add to my skill set to get myself a position at a
company that would be happy for me to grow?

One area I decided to focus on was building my network. I put
myself out there to network and find groups locally where I
could make connections. I was not from here, so I didn't
have a deep network of college friends or past coworkers to
call on. I had to go out and start fresh and meet new people,
so I spent a lot of time networking and attending meetups
and just trying to get to know people locally that could
possibly help me down the road.

As the previous stories highlight, your values, what you are capable of, and the bigger picture vision are pulling you, often in a new direction when you least expect it.

Doug Stitzer (Episode 035: Choosing Your Own Adventure Based on Your Strengths) specializes in using data processing technology to help financial services companies create world class, customer-centric experiences. He is currently the Director of Insurance at Salesforce. His pivotal moment comes from a season in his career when he took on a "choose your own adventure" approach and charted his own course based on his strengths.

Doug: *There comes a time when you outgrow your home. I was*
in a position where I was able to promote the idea of a
transformational change within my business. It was
approved by our board, and we moved forward with me
leading it. A couple of years into the project, our chief oper-
ations officer approached me and said, "Hey, I'm thinking
about making a career change for myself. Let's talk about
what that means for you." I'd been so heads-down working
on this program, leading some fantastic people with some
great change that was going to have a tremendous business
impact, I hadn't really focused on me. It was an emotional
moment when I went home that day and sat down and
talked with my wife and realized I was not excited for the

first time in my career about the next step being presented to me, so it started this period of soul-searching. I thought "I'm on the wrong side of 40 and I've got to figure out what I want to do when I grow up."

As I took that step back, I realized I'd done a good job of investing in my people and pushing them forward on their career path, but I had neglected myself, and it forced me to take stock of what was important, what motivated me to get up every day. Asking myself "What type of culture will I thrive in and what types of people do I want to be surrounded with?" ultimately led to this complete right-hand turn of determining to leave the traditional career side and move in more of an operations and technology role. It resulted in me coming back to my leader and saying, "I've got a different idea about how my gifts can be used in the organization." I proposed my own role and after about a year of going back and forth, negotiating my role, I raised my hand and said, "I don't think I have a home here. I'm willing to work on this until each of us feels that we need to part ways."

Trusting yourself requires an element of surrender. **Bridget Boyle (episode 030: Let Go to Grow)** is the Vice President of Human Resources, North American at Roche Diagnostics; she has had a significant impact on the organization through much growth and transition over the last several years. Her journey is one of intentionality and focus. She has developed the strength of redefining her value. Several years ago, she was presented with an opportunity to become the site head of Human Resources. It was an opportunity to expand her influence, but to ensure her success, she had to backfill her previous position—she had to let go of what she was really good at and step into something new.

>*Bridget:* *It sounded like an amazing opportunity, but it was one that I didn't really understand fully when it was presented to me. I had to learn how to let go of things, and it was one of the toughest professional transitions that I've ever gone through. It took me about eight months to a year to really get my head around what the new role was. What I found is that it was very hard for me to let go of what I knew and what I loved and what I was comfortable doing. I loved it so much. I knew the people. I knew the business. I knew it like the back of my hand and couldn't let go of that. And having to hand it over to someone on my team and say, "take good care of this business."*

>*The challenge for me was redefining what my value would be to the organization, redefining what my impact would be to the organization, so I answered these questions: Where will I spend my time? Who are my key stakeholders? What will my achievements look like as a leader in this new role? All of that had to be redefined. I finally learned a hard lesson of letting go and the magic and the beauty that can happen when you let go, because when you let go, you start to see opportunities, and that's what happened to me. The moment I let go I began to focus on this new role and where I can add value, I saw opportunities all over the place. And then it was no longer a question of "how will I demonstrate my value?" but instead, I had to choose what to focus on first.*

Each version of myself is being formed by past experiences and learnings. I am a better leader today having missed the mark as a leader. I am a better wife because of a failed marriage. I am a better mom having grown through the challenges. As Marianne Williamson says, "you must learn a new way to think before you can master a new way to be."

COACHING QUESTIONS

- How are you intentionally developing as a leader?
- What strategy(s) will you try on to proactively reinvent yourself?

5

HAVING A BIGGER PICTURE TO GO TO

*L*eadership development is not an event—it's an ongoing process, so the work never ends. **The best leaders are continuously doing the work** . . . the hard work of looking in the mirror at what's happening within them. THAT's where the power is.

Throughout the stories across the first year of *Being [at Work]*, leaders talked about gaining strength from something greater than themselves, and in each of those stories, they had something bigger to go to because they had done the work—they had taken the time to identify and name it. As I noted earlier, the theme is not about a particular format or structure (there are many ways to get there); the leadership practice to focus on is *going to* a shared bigger picture that everyone involved can rally around. That is the key for getting you and your team from chaos to clarity.

Thinking about the future comes naturally for many leaders. Others, who are more practical, struggle to think beyond what is. A pivotal moment for **Chris Byers, CEO of Formstack (Episode 037: Vision is Merely Stating What the Future Looks Like)** was realizing that it is vision (not a paycheck) that truly motivates team members. He kept finding himself frustrated with the results he was seeing, the way people were acting, and his inability to communicate what was in his head. A business coach asked him some critical questions: What is your 'why' statement? What is it about you that is likely going to be true no matter what job you're doing? What is the purpose that is in you, that you're going to play out in any role?

For Chris, the process of determining an organizational vision started with a vision for himself and what would NOT change. These reflection questions freed him up to think more broadly.

> **Chris:** It's important for me to understand what it is about me
> that's NOT going to change, even if I'm in a different job
> tomorrow. Once I discovered that, it gave me a foundation
> to start thinking about the future and what the vision could
> look like for Formstack.

We can easily overcomplicate going big-picture. No doubt, you have seen or experienced a 10-page strategic plan that sits in a binder, never to be used. To utilize the vision or our bigger-picture perspective, it must be accessible and digestible.

> **Chris:** Vision is merely stating what the future looks like. I
> always struggled with the idea of mission and vision. Those
> words sound very heavy. I never really thought of myself as
> a visionary.

So, building on his definition of "stating what the future looks like," he explored with his team.

> **Chris:** I asked my team to pretend like we are five years in the
> future. What are some true things you want to say about
> that moment in time? And then we named the characteris-
> tics of our team.

The value is in having a bigger picture to go to—being anchored to something. Because Chris engaged his team in this process, they shared in the bigger picture and could rally around it.

Brian Ahearn (Episode 043: Getting People to Say 'Yes') talks about the bigger picture that others can rally around as common language.

> *Brian: One of the things I learned a long time ago is to have a common language, especially within an organization, so that when you talk about things, everybody knows what you mean. When we began to incorporate new ideas into our sales training internally and then eventually externally with insurance agents who represented the company, we began to have a common language. We would say, "Okay, what does it mean to persuade?" Rather than having 10 different people come up with 10 different definitions, we were able to settle on a definition. Then we were able to take the psychology and use that as the basis for why we were going to ask the salespeople to change their behavior, because when they realized, for example, that if we do X, Y, Z, that will engage the principle of reciprocity. They've all been through training and they remember what reciprocity is. They've heard the studies and they know how powerful it can be to move people to action, so I think people got on board a lot sooner when that started happening.*

Right at the beginning of the COVID-19 shutdowns, I sat down with **Scott Nicholson (Episode 034: Leading in the Midst of the COVID-19 Crisis),** one of my business partners at HRD to unpack what had been helpful in leading through the challenge. Not surprising, Scott acknowledged the importance in having a bigger-picture plan to guide us throughout the challenge. At the beginning of the pandemic, we created a plan to outline different levels of activity—interactions with internal team members, how we will handle meetings and travel and clients, and it immediately brought a sense of clarity to the team. It provided direction about where we are and how we will adapt as things change and it gave us something to anticipate.

> *Scott: When you share a plan with your team, they see that
> you have made a concerted effort and a document that you
> are actively managing and decisioning from and that
> provides comfort. The minute there are mixed messages or
> confusion emanating from the top, then there is a high level
> of discomfort.*

Scott and I also acknowledge that, as things come up, you can go back to the plan to ensure consistency and alignment with your choices. This bigger-picture plan gave us something to rally around, so it drove cohesion within our leadership team.

I appreciate the opportunity to work with Scott as a business partner. The bigger-picture focus is consistent through his leadership. I have seen him in tricky situations, and he does not get sucked into the emotional muck. Instead, his resolve is steady. We worked together a couple of years ago to create and present a variable compensation plan to our team. Because of our team focus, our goals were to create a plan that both awarded individual leadership and overall organizational performance. When we first rolled it out to the team, we got pushback and a lot of questions. I found myself getting defensive, but followed Scott's lead. He asked questions to understand and continued to come back to the goal of incentivising both individual and team performance. Because of that goal, there were some gray areas within the plan, but because Scott had started with our why and the philosophy behind our approach, they bought in.

Scott and I often have the "meeting before the meeting." Anytime we are rolling something out to the team or getting their thoughts on something new, we take time *before* the meeting to align. It is important for the team to see the cohesion in our message, and the consistency in our "why" gives us the bigger picture to reiterate throughout the meeting (just as Scott did with the compensation plan).

Seth Morales (Episode 007: The Challenge of Change), CEO of Morales Group recognized division in his business several years ago because of lack of cohesion at the top. He recognized the impact this was having on the organization, so he led the charge on aligning the leadership team to a mission statement and a set of shared values.

> *Seth: We really started to plug into our core values and our mission statement. We had ten core values and we narrowed it down to three—be humble, be courageous, and be a light. Then, we refined our mission statement, which is "Building better futures one story at a time." We started to share that with the team. We had a monthly cadence, and we would bring everyone together to talk about those three core values and the mission statement. We started to notice a real difference in our business. People started to become more engaged. There was clarity with where we were going, and then the business in turn started to see benefits as well. We started to grow quite a bit in revenue. We went from $34 million in 2012 and today we are on a run rate to do $150 million. That was a really good educational experience for me to see. If you don't have cohesive leadership, you are going to struggle as a business.*

In Seth's example, it is clear they brought these foundational elements to life. They took time to define the big picture together as a team and make it actionable for team members. They didn't just identify core values; they brought them to life as values in action.

> *Seth: The single most important thing that we did was create our LEGOS program. LEGOS stands for Loving Every Gift of Service. Each month, team members nominate co-workers who have gone above and beyond the call of duty with our three core values. If somebody was courageous or humble or somebody was a light, they nominate them to our LEGOS email address; we collect the LEGOS nominations and then we share them with the team at a monthly huddle called our LEGOS meeting. Those who were nominated get an individual LEGO block and they end up building this home.*

There are these four walls that are built up over the course of the year. We engage monthly and intentionally get folks to think about it, and then when the four walls are built up and we're profitable enough as a company, we take a group to Mexico and build actual homes. That's been a really cool way to get buy-in. It creates a cadence and it's just a great way I think to intentionally develop and hone-in on your core values and ensure people are looking for your values.

Seth's example is an important reminder of the value of bringing the values to life in a way that engages all team members in the process. Imagine having an opportunity to serve others by building a home for them—and the opportunity exists just by being a good leader, demonstrating the core values of the organization. The values then become the norm for how we treat each other—that is the culture that Seth and his team have created at Morales Group.

In a different industry and market, **Jeff Wagner (Episode 039: Four Strategies for Leading Through Change)** drove cohesion within his team by using the foundation of a shared vision. Jeff was in a new role with a new team and was asked to completely overhaul their product development process, taking 50% of the time to market out of the process, which is significant. He confidently says that he didn't know what he was doing.

Jeff: It wasn't just about changing the time to market, which was important, but we also had a quality problem, so the first thing that we did was define goals and objectives; then, we got a cross-functional team involved. We had a shared vision with the rest of those team members around what it is that we were trying to achieve. We put it in terms that they could relate to and get on board with, so they couldn't argue with it. We said things such as, "What if we took 50% of the time out of the product development process? And what if the first time that you got a call on our product, you were prepared with a process and you knew what the service level agreements were? Would that be a good thing?"

> *There's no one in that room or on the team that could say no to that, and so you've established a shared vision. You've got them on board with what it is that you're trying to do. And then I found that reinforcing that over time, during the course of the project worked out well because we constantly reminded them, "Here's why we're here. This is what we're trying to accomplish." It drove engagement. I'd say foundationally, the most important thing was getting that shared vision and having the whole team in the same boat, rowing in the same direction.*

Jeff stayed on the stage by finding common ground. He mobilized the people that were most impacted by the change and got them to determine what it would look like going forward which created a high level of ownership.

Ryan Coon (Episode 046: Rebranding as a Catalyst to Rally the Team) is another example of rallying the team around a shared direction, and he did it through a rebranding effort.

> *Ryan: Starting a company and being an entrepreneur is truly a roller coaster. The highs are really high, and the lows are really low. I can remember the early days where we were so excited and wide eyed. We were pumped for every new day, and then there's the inevitable challenges where things don't work out. It's tougher than you imagined, and you just have to fight through those.*

One of those challenging moments for Ryan was recognizing a few years into the business that the brand no longer matched the service and the culture they were creating.

> *Ryan: People misconstrue branding as just your company name*

and company logo, and branding is so much more than that. It starts with taking stock of your core values and your purpose and your mission and why you do what you do and for whom. It's really all of those things, plus messaging, plus the name and the logo and the identity and the colors and all of that that really make up a brand. When you think about some of those top brands that we're all familiar with, whether it's Starbucks or Chipotle or Nike, they're so thoughtful about all of those different pieces, and we really had to take the time and take a step back and think about those things for ourselves and for our team and for our organization.

So, he led his team through a six-month process that started by looking internally. He likened it to individuals taking time to step back and reflect on who they are.

Ryan: It's almost identical to the process that we had to go through as an organization where we had to really take a step back and look at who we are. What do we value? What do we prioritize and really who do we want to be? Because, just like none of us want to go into a job that we hate, as a company we didn't want to build that company that no one likes. So for us, it was really taking a step back, figuring out: what do we value?

Today, we have four really critical core values that we talk about all the time as a team. We had to start thinking about who we are. Then, the next step in the process was talking with customers and understanding: what did they value in us? And then talking with our team and doing interviews with our team and understanding who they thought we were. And then once we did that, we were able to craft the values, the brand positioning, the brand messaging to determine a brand archetype. Only after you've uncovered all of that can you really start thinking about the fun stuff:

41

> *the name, the colors, the identity, the logo, and the font*
> *type.*

I highlighted earlier the symbiotic relationship between our challenges and our growth. Just like the challenges evolve as we evolve as leaders, as the organization evolves, the bigger picture evolves—it's all connected. **Adam Weber (Episode 051: Lead Like a Human)** is the Chief People Officer and co-founder at Emplify where he works every day to help people realize and activate their full potential. He has seen throughout his career how integrated and activated values have been the foundation of the organization's and team member success— employees know that success is not just *what* they do, it is *how* they do it.

Adam highlights how the values evolve as the organization evolves.

> ***Adam:*** *The core values have to be true. With all team members*
> *there is a process of really uncovering who you are and*
> *what makes your organization unique. You must determine*
> *what truly makes you who you are, do the work to uncover*
> *that and then leaning in and living that out is the number*
> *one way to bring new people into that. We celebrate people*
> *through those values. We recognize them. We promote. We*
> *hire based on those values, and we integrate situational*
> *questions to understand that those values are exhibited by*
> *the people that we hire.*

Earlier, I noted that going bigger-picture starts with you—it must because your leadership is a reflection of who you are. Always. Not sometimes. The impact that you have flows from the choices you make and how you show up and we set ourselves up to do that consistently when we've taken the time to identify who we are—what truly makes us who we are.

I saw firsthand many years ago the impact of NOT doing that. I worked for a CEO who had taken on someone else's values. The organization he was leading was founded on a very strong set of values that the founder integrated into the culture and became the foundation of all talent processes. The company grew rapidly, and the founder continually referenced the organization's values as the source of its strength. Upon joining the organization, each new team member went through an entire day called "culture day" in which the new employees explored the organizational values, what they meant to them, and how they played out in their leadership. The values were everywhere, and woven into the fabric of the organization.

When a new CEO was brought in to lead the organization's growth strategy, he espoused these values. He had a charming style and could turn it on when needed, but since the values were not authentically aligned with who he is as a leader, they lost their luster. As Adam says, the core values have to be true. In this case, they were not, and that created lack of trust and fear.

Not surprisingly, I saw a decline in that business over time. The CEO was surrounded by incredible talent which maintained a level of success for the organization, but his lack of authenticity was a constant source of challenge. This story is a reminder to check ourselves—*do my actions match my message?* Adam and his business partner checked themselves as their partnership evolved.

Prior to co-founding Emplify with his current business partner, Adam had founded and led another organization for four years, and they were fortunate enough to sell the company and kept almost all of the talent to start Emplify. Because the values had been so important in the previous organization, they realized that they needed to rethink the values of the new organization.

> **Adam:** *We asked ourselves, "Are they the same?' We went through this process of reimagining our values and reactivating them. One of the ways that was the most effective before we released them was to gather stories. Instead of asking, "What do you think of this value? What do you think of this value?" we asked them to share a story - a situation when this value was lived out. We asked them to name the person and tell the story. We went on this kind of*

story-collecting journey, and by the end, we had a full library of examples of the values already lived out before we even launched them. That gets to the essence of values— they should already be true. They already do exist. The key is to capture and collect those.

Adam describes the process of reimaging the values as a fun experience, as it was a second chance to work through the values with the same people. He describes the difference in determining values in a new organization and one in which the team has been working together for years.

Adam: *When we started the first business, it was very raw and authentic and we made those values sitting at his kitchen table. There wasn't formality and knowledge and we were not following a formalized process. But with Emplify, it was bigger than us. It wasn't just the two of us. We were incorporating cross departmental teams. We had the employees nominate one person from their department who already lives our values, the unknown future values. There were people from all levels inside the organization that participated and we all got together. We did a "hot pen" exercise, where you write about the culture five years in the future. You get 15 minutes to write about a specific day and time that really exemplifies the culture.*

That was the foundation of how we built and rediscovered those values; we listened to each of the narratives of the different people, and from there, the themes started to emerge. Then we determined which of the values we had noted could we make measurable to help someone know if they are living them out. From that, we created this core list, and how I know I'm living each of them, and we captured the stories, and once we had the stories, we launched.

There is a message across each of the stories in this section that reflects the individual leader's style and philosophy, and yet, in each of the stories, it was the pull of something bigger that kept the leader moving forward. Coming up from the muck of what is to explore something bigger gets us out of our own ego-driven head. The big picture is the key ingredient in staying on the stage. It provides a foundation and a reason to keep going.

COACHING QUESTIONS

- What is your relationship with your manager (or leaders that you report up to)?
- What strategy(s) will you try on to improve the relationship with your manager (or leaders that you report up to?

THEME II: FOCUS ON RELATIONSHIPS

"A beautiful thing happens when we start paying attention to each other. It is by participating more in your relationship that you breathe life into it."

— STEVE MARABOLI

6

POWERING UP THROUGH THE
RELATIONSHIPS

*L*eadership is a team sport. Leaders do themselves a disservice when they attempt to go it alone—as we're working towards our goal, it's important to recognize the strength of those around us. **The big picture can only be mobilized through our relationships**, so it serves us (and others) well when we focus on them.

My relationship with my colleague, Amanda, is a good example of the POWER in the relationship. As a leader, I get so much energy (as our business does) from my relationship with Amanda. She is the Vice President of Client Experience at HRD, and she leads our delivery team of coaches and facilitators ensuring a consistent level of excellent service to our clients. She does it all so well (as our clients will attest), while staying lock step with our sales and marketing teams. We are constantly communicating and if we haven't connected, I can count on a quick text or call to touch base. Amanda is a rock in our business— our relationship is built on mutual respect and a deep care and concern for each other. I trust her implicitly and know her heart for service and growth, so as her leader, the most important part of my job is enabling her to be successful. My business is successful and grows only to the level that my team is successful and growing. The results come from the team's success.

49

This is exactly why the transition to leader of people is a tricky one. Often in organizations, the strong individual contributor is promoted to manager because he or she is good at their craft. Unfortunately, being good at your craft does not translate into being a good manager, and yet organizations fall into this promotion trap repeatedly.

In my first role as an HR assistant, I was one of four HR assistants within the organization. We each reported up to an HR Manager, and I remember a perpetual sense of competition between us (largely driven by the competitiveness of the HR Managers). My goal was to be the best HR assistant and outperform the others. I was helping to administer our stock option program in collaboration with one of the HR Assistants, Maria, and remember purposefully withholding information from her because I wanted the credit for the good work, and my selfish behavior paid off. When a Senior HR Assistant position opened up, I was given the role. For the first time, I had individuals reporting to me, and suddenly found myself in a position in which I no longer got results on my own. Because of the relationships I had built with the team, I found this first transition went smoothly, as I led more as a buddy than a boss. Throughout my career, I have worked to create a strong friendship with my team members (knowing who they are is important to me). This worked in my initial leadership role, but proved much more difficult when I was promoted into another role.

I had been with the organization for about 18 months when a new HR leader was brought in to evolve our department. I was thrilled about the change, as I recognized the importance of evolving our outdated function. The new leader quickly established a direction for our department, one that required talent to step up into much more of a partnership role with the business. It was a refreshing change.

Within a few months of his joining the organization, we collaborated on the development of a new team within the HR department: the Learning and Performance Improvement Team. It was an opportunity to centralize learning and development across this global organization, and I was promoted to lead this team. I went into the role wide-eyed, with a focused vision.

But I made a critical mistake. I pushed my vision prior to building relationships with my new team. Gwen, Pat, and Tom had worked as sales trainers in the business for many years and were highly regarded experts. I couldn't understand why they didn't celebrate the new direction. Upon reflection, I recognize that I did not take the time to get to know them or build a relationship with them. I recognize now that I was threatened by their years of tenure – I felt like if I left them alone it would show that I trusted them. My hands-off approach, however, kept me from truly understanding what was happening with them, so I failed to establish a *shared* vision, and instead my vision and our efforts remained siloed. We never did get into a rhythm as a team. I worked very closely with the HR leader and collaborated with him but did not rally the troops.

It is an important leadership lesson in my journey, and I am grateful for the experience (and owe Gwen, Pat, and Tom an apology). We were in different regions across the country, and I remember once, in an effort to bring the team together, I hosted a team building session in Chicago where I was based. We walked along Lake Michigan, had a great dinner and some drinks, and strategized. Still, it fell flat. There was no momentum following that event. Team building and fancy dinners will never replace one-on-one time getting to know each other. That was my miss. I attribute my failure to continuing to do things the way I always had: on my own.

The difference between an individual contributor and a leader is simple: leaders get results *through* others. The transition can be difficult for many, because they underestimate how their mindset and behaviors need to shift in a leadership position. I did not recognize this in my first managerial position, and I struggled as a result. A study from the Ken Blanchard Company reports that 60% of new managers fail or underperform in their first two years, and much of the time it is because they have not been equipped to get results through others.

A few years into the leadership of this newly formed team, we semi-merged with another global team that was focused more broadly on organizational effectiveness, and I worked closely with Michael and Linda from this team. As I reflect on the difference in how I worked with them, it is night and day. I developed deep relationships with both Linda and Michael and our work product reflected that. Two teams with a very different vibe and very different outcomes; the difference was my level of relationships and the time I spent nurturing those.

At the heart of getting results through others is the relationship, and in each of our guests' stories, there is continual focus on the relationship more than the outcome of the result. We need each other. This chapter is an encouragement to focus on the people you lead—your key stake-holders—recognizing their humanness and what makes them tick.

Building strong relationships is the secret to getting results, and yet this can be a tough lesson to learn. The typical leadership path includes time as an individual contributor, so employees develop "me-focused" behaviors based on individual results. This is the trap that I fell into with the team I was trying to rally.

Many of our guests over the last year have shared similar lessons learned. **Matt McHatten (Episode 028: The Stages of Leadership – From 'It's all About Me' to CEO)** is the CEO at MMG Insurance, and he learned, from his father's advice and his early experience, the difference between leading and transacting.

> *Matt: My father told me starting out in my career, "Don't step on anyone on the way up the ladder, you may meet them coming back down," and that was a key element. Obviously, as a young, aggressive banker, that was important, but more so it was a statement on making sure that I regarded everyone. For instance, if you're going into a business, make sure you engage with everybody on your way through to meet with the owner or the leader of the business, and develop relationships as deeply as you can, because you never know. That was really great advice.*
>
> *Early in my career, it was all about me in terms of the harder I worked, the more success I had. I was in a commercial lending corporate finance role and it was all about produc-*

tion. I attributed a lot of success to working hard and producing, but that created a lot of bad habits that, along the way, I've had to work to correct, because I was very focused on production, and at times that's not the most important mode to be in as a leader. I thought I was leading, but actually I was transacting, and I was lucky in terms of the next phase of my career to report to an individual that provided me depth and the distinction of the two—distinction between leading and transacting.

Matt's story highlights the transition from individual contribution to leader—from getting results on your own to getting results through others. As he progressed in his career, he recognized the value in the relationship to drive production.

Kent Kramer (episode 004: Building Trust) also learned early in his career the value of building relationships at all levels. Kent is the CEO of Goodwill of Central and Southern Indiana and he says that getting to know people at all levels drives him on a daily basis. He adopted this leadership philosophy early in his career during a pivotal situation. In the mid-90's, he was working as a store manager for Sam's Club and was transferred to Washington D.C. He had asked for a challenge and did not realize just how challenging it would ultimately be.

Kent: It was just a different environment. Two weeks into the job, I discovered that the individuals in that store (who had just gone through a merger with another organization that acquired them) had decided to go forth with a union campaign and they started signing cards. Talk about a challenge—I was twenty-five years old and was in this new environment and had a union campaign going on, and it was the first ever that ended up being an actual election.

There was a spotlight on me, that store, and the people in that store. There were a lot of lessons learned. I do learn and I listen, and in this particular case, I had about three hundred employees in my store, and because of the union environment and knowing that we were going to an election, I had to get to know those folks really closely, and did that, and what I discovered was fascinating people and I can think back fondly on many of them. They were just trying to figure out how to survive. Many of them were working two and three jobs, using public transportation, living in neighborhoods that weren't safe, and they were truly in survival mode. It gave me an appreciation, as I hadn't grown up in that environment. I didn't see that environment in college. This was my first couple of years of professional experience, and it gave me an appreciation that I've never forgotten. To this day, I appreciate and have empathy for individuals at all levels no matter the case, and this was a case of a heated environment. I recognized that they were just trying to take care of their families and trying to figure out what to do.

Having a passion for people drives a need to build relationships, particularly in the midst of a tough situation. **Philip Mann (episode 003: Rebuilding Your Team)** is the Senior Director at Macy's Logistics Operations. When Philip joined Macy's he quickly realized that there was a culture issue within the facility he was working in that stemmed from the disengagement of his senior team, so he went to work rebuilding the team by talking to people.

Philip: *People require nurturing and if they know it's present and they know it's safe and there is trust, they get there. People need good leadership, and if they have it, people are incredibly tenacious at striving toward an objective that they share. It's staying connected to people, Andrea. It's staying connected all the way back down to the floor. We cannot let the demands of the business take us away from the purpose of the business—from the heart of the business, and that's the people.*

Both Philip's and Kent's stories highlight the value in people... *all* of the people. That is where the meaning comes from. There is no business without the people leading it. In each of their stories, it is clear that they have a heart for lifting others up.

I am grateful to my parents for perpetually lifting me up throughout my life—I see the tremendous impact of their influence in all I do. My mom and dad are both sources of strength, particularly in the challenging times. In 2004, I was going through a divorce and struggling to find my footing. My dad wrote me a letter that I will keep for the rest of my life. I pull it out on occasion when I need a boost. He begins the letter in his matter-of-fact way: "Consider all of your positive qualities." He called out what he saw in me, and listed over and over the strengths that would undoubtedly lead me through that tough time in my life and beyond. And he was right.

Circa 1980 – on my Dad's shoulders; he has always lifted me up.

I attribute much of my self-confidence to my dad's influence. I grew up with two older brothers, and he let me get gritty like the boys. I don't ever remember feeling like I wasn't up for an adventure or challenge because I was a girl – playing sports with a group of boys, rough housing were normal parts of my experience – it never dawned on me that I couldn't do something. Both of my parents always encouraged me to try and do it all; my dad encouraged me to take risks, try new things, and speak my heart. He encouraged my voice. That is what he has always done. One of my favorite pictures of us is me as a little girl on his shoulders because it's a metaphor for our relationship: he is always lifting me up. If I need a boost, my dad and my mom are there to boost me.

Tammy Butler (Episode 053: The Work Goes On) also recognizes the value in lifting others. She leads her organization with a purpose as she taps into the value and expertise in leaders at all levels. She encourages organizations to challenge their talent processes to ensure that they assess the whole person, not just the information presented on the resume.

> *Tammy: You have to search for those diamonds in the rough. Previously, whenever we had a job posting, we would automatically make an assumption that there was no one in the organization that could fill the role, and that was based on our own preliminary scan that we would do of individuals, so we would post on Indeed and other job sites. One day, one of our contact leaders came to us about a data analytics position we were trying to hire and said, "Hey, the role that you're trying to fill, I think there's someone in our contact center that can do it. I think that they can fill that particular role." We were appreciative of that and asked them to send their resume over and talk with HR to see if there is a fit, and if so, we'd get them an interview. Sure enough, this person sent their resume over and we were absolutely amazed at the experience this person had. And they were in our contact center. It was an employee who had already gone through a stint at work and had retired, but after being in retire-ment, had decided that they really wanted to come back into the workforce. When they came back into the work-*

force, they brought all this experience that they previously had.

> *We were seeing that person as someone in our contact center, which is normally an entry-level role, and assuming that everyone that was there was entry-level. Based on this experience, we decided we were going to start posting internally first for all of these positions that we would be hiring to fill various projects or for staff augmentation. It was amazing what we started finding out about people—we had recruiters, and people with data analytics skills, and we had nurses that were in the organization. Sometimes because of the position that someone applies for and accepts, because of whatever backdrop that might exist, then you put them in that box and think that they are an entry-level employee, they met the qualifications for the job, but in reality, there is much more to that person that's sitting there, either receiving or making that telephone call.*

> *Now we do a skills analysis when a person comes so we know the skills that exist as we have other positions that come up or we're sourcing for other projects; we want to identify people in our organization that have the skillset and potential. In this way, we can cultivate what they already have as a starting foundation to propel them to the next level. We're tapping into the talent right in front of us. We're out spending lots of money on job sites and recruiting fees, and we have folks that are sitting right here, literally right under our noses.*

Tammy's story highlights the impact that focusing on people has on employee engagement and retention. Similarly, **Rick Cardwell (Episode 011: Owning Your Story)**, Vice President and Head of Midwest Region at Infosys focuses on the individual. His philosophy is taking each person as they come and being willing and able to really hear each person's story.

Rick: Ultimately, for the people who have worked for me, the most important thing is whether or not they became better human beings. When I first became a manager, there were 13 people on the team and every year they would go through these corporate surveys. As I read through the surveys, the results didn't help me because it didn't provide insight on what makes an individual employee tick, what motivates them, or how they emotionally connect to their job.

I did some research because I personally think these corporate surveys are watered down and generalized, so I looked for very personal questions that would give me the insight I was looking for, questions such as: "Do you have a best friend at work?" "Have you been complimented in the last seven days?" "When was the last time you and your manager sat down and talked about your performance?" I looked at questions that included time-based interactions and were more focused on individual employee answers rather than collective responses. And as a result, I started to notice that the strengths and weaknesses of an individual at their workplace translates to their personal life, because all of them would share their personal story.

It clicked in me that if I can figure out how to motivate them relative to their needs and how to help improve their perfor-mance in the workplace, that invariably will translate them into becoming better human beings because they will apply the same tools in their personal life. That is where the reward is for me. That's what I keep in front of me now, is that connecting point that understands that they're just not employees; they're also human beings, being at work.

There's a particular situation that stands out to Richard in which this philosophy plays out.

Rick: We have recruited people from all over the United States with various backgrounds. We hired an individual right out of college, who went through some very intensive training and the stress and anxiety of moving from his hometown, away from his family into a brand new city and brand new job and he started to express his anxiety through cutting his arms. To relieve the anxiety, he would cut on his forearms. The team members in his training class recognized this becoming a trend and they reached out to our human resources department and me as well to notify us as this trend is happening. It was obviously a disruption to the workplace, as people are concerned and it's a distraction, so we sat down and had a one-on-one conversation with him, just to understand what was happening and how we could help him.

He started sharing that he came from a dysfunctional, broken home. He was the first person in his family to graduate from college and he was having a hard time acclimating. In listening to him, I realized that we had similar backgrounds: I'm the first person in my family to go to college. There was a period of time when I was in sixth grade, I was homeless. My parents were divorced. They abused alcohol and drugs and were gone, so I slept in the car and showered in the gym before school started each day. I shared that story with this struggling team member to connect and personally relate to what he was going through. At my level, people assume you got there because you worked hard, you came from a good family and you didn't have a lot of major setbacks in your life. I encouraged him to not be ashamed of his background but instead, to own it. That's who you are and that's a part of your story, and you need to put that in front of people — that way, you own the narrative and not them. The conversation ended with my reinforcing that I want you to be here and I want you to know that you're cared for and want you to be a part of the team.

I'm happy to say that since that conversation, he has gotten the help he needs and we haven't seen any evidence of cutting. Knowing that he doesn't have a solid support system outside of the workplace, we invariably, by default, have become that support system for him. We have become the consistent voice. We have become the mentor and have embraced his strengths, his weaknesses and are willing to continue giving him a chance and molding him. There's a tremendous amount of pride, I think we have in that because it wasn't about his technical ability, it was about his ability to be happy and a healthy human being.

There's no such thing as leaving your stuff at the door. Whenever anyone engages in their week, they are doing so with all of the "stuff." We can't separate the person from the employee, so we are best served by supporting the whole person.

When I worked for the national security company, I learned a practice that I still use today: starting team meetings with "positive focus." Rather than jumping into the business at hand, it was a requirement in that organization to begin every meeting with positive focus—each person briefly sharing a personal and professional positive—something good that was happening in their life or something they were grateful for. This practice ensures that we begin the meeting with connection and knowing what is happening in the lives of the people we work with. It sets a positive tone for the meeting and engages everyone right out of the gate.

In an emotional conversation with **Val Tate (Episode 044: Racism Hurst Us All: How Do We Lead Better)** on the heels of the George Floyd murder in Wisconsin, she shared a story that highlights power of coming together.

Val: You can't hurt someone without hurting yourself. It is not possible. I believe that racism hurts white people too. It is narcissistic to teach your child that they are better than someone else based on race. You see a child grow up thinking this, and when they become a certain age they realize that it's not true. Being better than someone else is in conflict with your soul knowledge. If you have any kind of spirituality that teaches certain principles, edicts, rules, laws or whatever that that person has to anguish in regards to that; they have to.

Val saw this anguish firsthand. Many years ago, she worked with a woman who did all kinds of little things to her. Val refers to them as "nasty little things."

Val: I really didn't know her, so I couldn't really understand why; she just kept doing things, gaslighting kinds of things. So, one day I asked her, "Why are you doing this?' and she left me alone for a bit, and then one time, we were in a training session together and this woman broke down crying and told me that her father was a racist and that he had taught her certain things about black and brown and people of color, and it hurt her. I saw how it was for her to have to learn that that wasn't so. For example, I'm a go-getter. I don't let up, and if I want something, I'm going to go after it. Imagine having to work with someone and you have been told your whole life that they're this certain way —lazy, having kids out of wedlock, and all of these negative things, and then you work with someone who is the exact opposite of what you've been taught about these people. She battled with me, and I had to train her. I had to teach her, and I wasn't happy about it.

I appreciate Val's courage in asking her coworker the question, "Why are you doing this?" That forced her to look in the mirror.

61

Val worked through this incredible challenge with her coworker.

> **Val:** *We have the opportunity to never have to come back here again. We have an opportunity to live a life, a freedom that we've never had before. And by the way, the young lady that I wrestled with, today we are the best of friends. We do the work together and facilitate conversations on race.*

Val's key message is this: **All healing happens within the relationship.**

Brene Brown says "it's hard to hate people up close." Val had the courage to get close and it led to a friendship that has now grown into teaching others.

> **Val:** *Up close means: "I read you. I see you. I see your hurt. She struggled, as did I, because I don't want to hate either. I don't see any reason to hate what hates me. I don't want to hate anybody."*

Hating does not feel good—ever. Val leaned into it—I will never know what it feels like to walk in her shoes and how hard that must have been. Imagine if we all leaned into the discomfort and asked, "Why are you doing this?" In doing so, she cracked open a door and brought light to a dark situation.

Our overhead light was out in our first floor living room, so I brought a lamp to the living room from our basement that doesn't get used very often. It had been in an area in our basement where there is plenty of light, so it doesn't get turned on very often, and yet when I brought it up into a room that needed light, suddenly my family noticed it and asked, "Did we get a new lamp? Where did that lamp come from?" I told them that we had always had this lamp; we had not been using it. By bringing it into a dark room, suddenly there was much more opportunity for the light.

The same can be said about our leadership during a challenging time. It's easy to lead through the good things. It's when the going gets tough that we have the greatest opportunity to support, align, and encourage those around us.

I have always been a fan of the band U2. My uncle is a super-fan, so I've grown up listening to their music. Seeing them in a concert is certainly on my bucket list, and I appreciate the way in which their lead singer, Bono, has given back and shown leadership throughout his career. He once said, "Whenever you see darkness, there is an extraordinary opportunity for the light to burn brighter." His message is a call to pay attention to the need; where there is need, there is opportunity.

In the awareness of the dark moments, there is an opportunity for leaders to bring light to the situation, just as Val did, and the other leaders we've highlighted in this book. We add value when we reach for a light-bearing thought or action, such as acknowledging the dark parts, offering support, validating how someone is feeling, sharing an encouraging word or a smile, offering an ear to simply listen... All of these actions bring light to the situation and create a shift which is an important part of going big picture, stepping into and staying in the tough moments, and focusing on the relationship.

COACHING QUESTIONS

- What are the key relationships in your life?
- What strategy(s) will you try on to nurture and grow these relationships while building up and adding light to these lives?

7

BEING INTENTIONAL

A common sentiment I have felt, particularly early in my career, is: "I don't have time to build the relationship—I have to get results." Achiever is one of my top strength themes—I like to get stuff done. I get energy from a sense of accomplishment.

What I have learned over the years is that the results are not sustainable or meaningful *without* the relationship of those involved with you in the task or activity; that is where meaning comes from. Early in my career, I co-led a global initiative with my colleague, Michael, to implement the organization's first online learning system. Michael has a gift of quickly connecting with people. His likeability is off the charts as he has a natural curiosity and wit that disarms and builds trust instantly.

As we traveled around the UK, meeting with leaders within different business units, I noticed that he always led with the relationship: getting to know the leaders we were working with and/or building on the relationship he had, asking questions about their goals, opportunities, and challenges. It wasn't about implementing the new online learning system. His focus was on the people we were meeting with and those they led: their frustrations and challenges. I still have the set of notes from the many meetings we had over the course of several days; I kept the notes all of these years as a reminder of this experience and all that I learned. It was a week I will always hold dear as it was an incredible lesson in leadership and what's most important. While I don't remember the words that were said (I can, however, see them in my notes), I can instantly recall the tone of those meetings. I remember how they felt: there was openness and curiosity; I drew smiley faces in my notes. While we were introducing something new that many had no experience with, there was energy, because of the focus on the relationships.

As my friend, Tim Robinson says, "Before you do any education, build the relationship." That is what my colleague Michael modeled for me.

When our mindset shifts to "relationship-driven results," the time challenge dissipates because the path to get results is *through* the relationship. It is the choices we make each day, the little things we choose to do for the people in our lives that make a difference. This is something I've learned as I've matured as a leader and that is largely because of the impact of the relationships.

Several years ago, I co-founded an organization called Next Gen Talent with my friend and business partner, Kelly Lavin. The organization was founded on our shared passion for the development of business skills in early-career HR and talent leadership.

Since starting the development program, the organization has been incorporated as a non-profit business, we have strategically established a group of leaders to serve on the board of directors and are building a strong team to execute the day to day operations of the program. Most importantly, we have evidence of growth across the participants–influencing their businesses in new ways with the new skills they have learned. While there is much work to be done, there is great success and as I reflect on the attributes of our success, the thing I believe to have added the most value is my relationship with Kelly.

As we were establishing the organization, we met once a week for breakfast–this focused time allowed us to co-create with intentionality and alignment. We are partners and have a relationship based on mutual trust and respect and a shared vision. We have a strong foundation from which to execute our goals. We are very different and leverage our differences as a source of strength for the business.

Karen Alter's (Episode 026: The Big Impact of the Little Things) story is another great example of the impact of our work relationships. Karen is the CEO and partner at Borshoff, an Indianapolis based full-service communications agency. Karen has also prided herself on work relationships and work friendships. Her experience has shown that the level of relationship directly influences the work the team can create together and the results the team can achieve. She is passionate about her work. And just when life felt so on-track, she got some big news that could have knocked her off-track. But because of the relationships, support and confidence of her work family at Borshoff, she not only led through the challenge with a lot of grace, she also emerged a stronger leader and has used the challenging experience to shape how she leads today.

In 2010, she says she was at the top of her game, doing work she loved and firing on all cylinders, and as part of a routine medical exam, her doctors discovered that she had colon cancer.

> **Karen:** *Over the course of that year, I was pretty sick off and on. I had to do both chemo and radiation, and it stopped me in my tracks. What I was overwhelmed by was the support from my Borshoff family. The team members ebbed and flowed with what I needed. We provide client service, so providing client service is priority number one, trying to keep them happy and work towards their goals. It's a challenge when you're fully healthy, so the support that was provided me from the leadership ownership down to administrative support was incredible. Where people stepped in, they stepped up. We never missed a beat with any of my clients. It was amazing that I could kind of come in and out based on how I was feeling. If I was having a good day, I was doing my thing and I was really contributing, and then other days, if I needed to not be reachable, I wasn't. That flexibility and that support was just truly amazing.*

Karen attributes the strengths of the relationship to the culture at Borshoff.

> **Karen:** *I think it's the culture we have here. We take a partner-ship approach, not only with each other, but with our clients, and we have to have that reliability in order to share common goals, so I think that came through. It was very well exhibited, in my personal experience.*
>
> *I also think that I am a very relational person; I wear all my feelings on my sleeve and my relationships are key. I'd been there for 13 years and I have really good friends. I am with these people a lot and we go through a lot of highs and lows and big things and little things. My relationships were so strong and so deep that there was a true passion and care, genuine care for me and for each other. There wasn't any struggle through that at all. There might have been, but they just never shared it with me. It seemed very seamless.*

Karen goes on to say that it was the little things that had the biggest impact on her, whether it was a text letting her know they were thinking of her, a card in the mail, or even a meal or a teddy bear dropped off by a coworker.

> **Karen:** *One day I was sort of starting to feel like I could do some work, and when I turned my iPAD on, there was this really fun message – a video message with music. There were a lot of little things like that. Our team is so creative, so they always want to take something and make it really special. It was fun to receive those different things through different channels. Just right what I needed at the right time.*

Dave Neff (Episode 031: The Unique Blend of Stewarding Relation-ships and Relentless Execution) is the Chief Revenue Officer at Prolific. He recognizes the impact that his relationships have had on his career journey, and is intentional about building and maintaining relationships.

> **Dave:** *I've been fortunate. A lot of amazing people have seen something in me and have chosen to invest in me, and I have really tried to steward those relationships. I read a book in my first year at the Pacers called* Never Eat Alone *by Keith Ferrazzi. It was all about building success one relationship at a time, and I have really tried to be a caretaker of the relationships in my life.*
>
> *If I meet you for coffee or for a meal, I will jot down just a few key things in my contact for you in my phone or on my laptop, so when I see you three, six months, or a year from now, it can jog my memory. We aren't superhuman, and I don't have a photographic memory, but I can go the extra mile and jot a few notes down to document those conversations. It's helpful to have a system to leverage that so when I see that person again in six months or a year, it can feel very genuine and authentic, even though I don't have that memorized by heart.*

We can't possibly build deep relationships with everyone, so how do we go about determining who to build relationships with? **Deborah Wintner's (Episode 047: Insights from a Seasoned Practitioner of Change)** story highlights the importance of knowing WHO your key stakeholders are; she also notes the importance of focusing first on the relationship. Deborah Wintner is Vice President, Human Resources for STANLEY Security and she highlights this as something she learned as she was transitioning into organizations.

> **Deborah:** *It was a lesson learned that I really had to dig in and build my relationships first instead of digging in because I had the answers and I'd seen this movie before. I knew what plays we should run."*

By building trust first, she developed the credibility to best influence the organization. During our conversation, I asked Deborah how specifically she has gone about building relationships.

> **Deborah:** *As I've transitioned to different roles in my career, one of the first things that I do is to really get a pulse from my manager and from my team on who the key stakeholders are; then, I put a 90-day plan together outlining the critical cross-functional leaders in the business. Then, I establish regular one-on-one meetings as a learning opportunity focused on getting to know this person, learning about our go to market strategy and what impacts our bottom line, identifying the key levers in the organization that impact our ability to influence the external markets, and determining the greatest opportunities.*
>
> *The key is to ask the questions about the business and then follow up on your conversation as you think about the business and the people strategy, what's working today that we need to continue to leverage and where do we have opportunities."*

This provides a structured approach for building new relationships. Deborah's intentional focus on the right people and the right activities is the key that set her up for success.

Sundaresh Ramanathan (Episode 038: Applying Feedback) has spent much of his career leading engineering operations and has learned the value of leveraging multiple perspectives to get to the best solution.

> **Sundaresh:** *The solution comes from a variety of sources. It's like a jigsaw puzzle. You start with a small piece of the puzzle and then you just keep building on. You keep adding to it. Within the team, the different individuals see different scenarios because of past experiences, or they just have a different perspective. And through discussion and putting all of the pieces together, you end up with a pretty picture.*

At the time of our recording, Sundaresh was in the process of building an app for a customer with his team. He said, "I have ideas on how it should be built," but he kept those to himself. One of his engineers who was leading the charge led a meeting with seven other talented engineers and instead of offering solutions, he shared the problem that they were trying to solve.

> **Sundaresh:** *We ended up with seven different solutions, seven different ideas, which made the overall offering that we ended up taking to the customer so much better than what I had started out with, and now we're all super excited that we're going to be able to take this awesome solution to the customer.*

Not only did they have a fuller solution to offer to the customer but engaging the team in the solution also had a big impact on them because they feel like they're a part of it. This story is at the heart of getting results through others. As Sundaresh noted, leveraging each perspective within the team benefited the customers' external relationships.

Phil Daniel's (Episode 027: Building a Business that Lasts – Service is the Thread) story also highlights the impact of internal relationships and connection on the customer. Phil is the President at JDA Worldwide. As he was building Springbuk, a health analytics solution for mid to large-sized employers, their core value of "Win Together" encouraged everyone to sacrifice their own goal for the team, and this was key to their significant growth. He describes how that played out in the organization.

> **Phil:** *Our primary core value is Win Together, and that suggests a lot of things. Most notably, it's collaboration. In the early or mid-stage of the cycle that we're in, we have to work across the line. Whether it's marketing and sales being aligned, whether it's marketing and product being aligned, whether it's engineering and our data, things being aligned across the business, we need transparency*

and we need everybody to understand the critical role and working together and helping each other, even be willing to sacrifice their own good or their own goal for the betterment of the business in some cases. That is a big, big deal to us. This idea of collaboration and winning together, and what's fun about that value is that it extends outside of the business. That mindset drives how we serve our clients.

One of my favorite stats from the business over the last 18 months is that over one-third of our new features and releases within the software within the product come directly from customer feedback. We have built a system that allows us to listen to them, to get their share of voice and to really just make sure we're capturing their needs and what they need to be successful, and that's winning together. It's not just Springbuk closing the sale or moving on. It's all of us buying in and solving this larger prevention and health care problem together.

It's easy for entrepreneurs or as a growing company to think that you have the answers and you have this this thing called a roadmap. You think you have this pulse from the market and you always want to be innovating and staying ahead of competitors, and the temptation is not to listen to customers in the market. That's one area where we've really improved in the last couple of years is to understand, you know, the customer voice and to really be an advocate for them to say what do you need to be successful? It's been a really key part of our growth.

Throughout each of these stories, there is intentionality on prioritizing the relationship. When that exists, we all win, but it takes discipline and often going against the grain of the short-term focus, urgent work environment.

My colleague, Amanda, navigates this challenge well. With each team member she onboards, she goes above and beyond to build the relationship as she is enabling the new team member to be successful in his or her role. She devotes hours to 1:1 conversations, asking questions, giving focused feedback, and talking through opportunities. She also makes sure to spend time with the new team member out of the office, even including them in family dinners. This focus on the relationship builds trust and credibility so she is able to engage in tough conversations with much more confidence and clarity.

COACHING QUESTIONS

- How are you being intentional about the key relationship in your life?
- What strategy(s) will you try on to better leverage your key relationships?

8

BUILDING TRUST

*M*y colleague, Amanda's example in being intentional to build relationships with new team members highlights the power of trust in the relationship. Trust builds the foundation for tough moments and tough conversations to exist.

Throughout my career, I've hired talented people who often ended up struggling in their first year or two in the new role, particularly when it's a stretch role. I've learned through failures that the key in the challenging moments is to acknowledge what is. It's not as much about solving the problem as it is being willing to acknowledge the challenge; that is the first step. Good communication is at the heart of any strong relationship. There is tremendous power in having the tough conversations and sharing what's on your heart and mind.

My best friend, Jessica, recently offended me at the end of an evening after we'd had dinner and some drinks. I was driving home and wanted to have an early night because of a busy day I had planned the following day, but she wanted to stay out, and was giving me a hard time for wanting to head home early. It triggered something in me, something that I've felt before but never told her about. So a few days later, I called her and acknowledged how her comments had landed.

She listened and apologized and we both talked through what we could learn from that situation. Our relationship is stronger because of the level of openness and transparency. We both trust each other to share our whole hearts, and the relationship benefits as a result.

I struggle to bring this level of transparency and openness into other relationships, and as I have reflected on what it is that holds me back, I have come to realize that what's missing is the high level of trust I feel with Jessica.

So how can leaders create an environment that is psychologically safe? How can we create an environment that is transparent and open? There are some good insights in our guests' stories.

Joe Barrett (Episode 023: Transparency in the Performance of Your Team) is the Vice President Sales and Marketing at DuraMark Technologies. Joe has a reputation for bringing a high level of integrity to the senior-level sales positions he's held throughout his career. He is candid in sharing his perspective. He believes that at any given time, your team members should be able to ask "where am I?" regarding their performance and understand your perspective on how they're doing.

> *Joe: The pivotal moments in my career have taught me the importance of being transparent and honest. Simply put, I've come to realize that people work so hard and if you hire talented people, they deserve to understand your opinion of that work that they do every day.*
>
> *Being successful includes having difficult conversations, exciting conversations, and happy conversations. Most important is to be honest with yourself and honest with the people around you, and that can take on many different facets and take in many different directions.*

Joe admits that giving honest feedback isn't something that comes naturally to him.

> *Joe: I forced myself at some point along the way to step out of my comfort zone. The comfort zone is "Don't say anything; don't have this conversation, avoid," but at some point early in my career, I forced myself to step outside of my comfort zone, and that's what I would suggest to new leaders, because it's just the right thing to do.*

Joe goes on to share an example from many years ago when he stepped outside of his comfort zone when working through a performance issue with a team member. He decided not only to give verbal feedback, but also to visualize the performance gap to ensure that the talk track matched the conversation and the feedback. He drew a line and said, "Here's how we perform as individuals." He says that whether it's a bell-shaped curve or a straight line really doesn't matter.

> *Joe: Typically in an organization, 5 to 15 percent of your people will be underperforming on a project, or in general, 70 percent will be successful, and then the remaining 5 to 15 percent are going to be exceptional performers. So, I will literally draw a line representing the team's performance and then ask the team member to do the same thing. Then, without showing each other, we both put a mark on the line representing the team member's performance. By doing that, it forces honest conversation, and in my experience, the words spoken up to that point may or may not line up to where we assessed visually.*

> *This is an open, honest, and helpful way to kick off the conversation. I believe that any leader should be able to do that at any point in time, throughout the year or throughout a project lifecycle, to let somebody know how they're doing and to ensure alignment in their perspectives. It can be such a good visual of your level of alignment or misalignment. Often, what we have been saying is not matching what we're seeing, so this forces the conversation.*

Another example of creating a safe environment in which to give honest feedback comes from **Matt Odum (Episode 012: The Value of Giving Honest Feedback)**, President of Briljent. Matt has learned that developing his team is his number one job as he runs the business. During our conversation, he talked about a situation which high-lighted for him the value of giving honest feedback. It didn't unfold the way in which Matt thought it would initially, which ended up being a great leadership lesson for him. The situation occurred four years into his role as President of the organization.

> **Matt:** *I had an executive team member that I had not set clear expectations for. As she was growing in her career, I had not helped her and equipped her with the tools and the skillset to meet the growing expectations of somebody in her role within a growing company.*

Matt engaged with a consultant to do a 360 review with this executive team member and expected his feedback to be somewhat disguised amongst a group of feedback.

> **Matt:** *I answered questions more honestly than I would have otherwise if I had known that my name was going to be attached to that feedback. My answers would have been different—they would have been the answers of an imma-ture leader that wasn't ready to be in his position at that point. Fortunately, accidentally, that wasn't the case. So, within this 360-degree assessment, I gave this radically honest feedback that proved challenging for the executive team member to receive.*
>
> *She was pissed off at me for two to three days and didn't voice that. To our benefit, and to the company's benefit, she and I have a very trusting relationship which likely caused it to be a bit more painful at first, and a little bit easier later. When I realized that my radically honest feedback had*

gotten to her desk, I felt a lot of guilt over it because it wasn't intentional.

However, the benefit of that has been proven since. After two to three days of her getting this feedback, we finally sat down to talk through it with the consultant and she facilitated the discussion. It ended up being not only a pivotal point for me around the value of honest feedback in my relationships with my direct reports, but it was also a pivotal moment in my personal relationship with this leader. Once we got through this, and it wasn't easy, and we moved into the process of correcting some of the challenges, we aligned priorities with the business priorities, and today, there is no other leader with whom I hold this level of trust and respect. It has been a huge benefit to the business as a whole because we're efficient and don't worry about the noise or the stuff that often comes with executive relationships. There is so much trust and respect and it would be very tough to crack that.

Because of Matt's openness in leading through the situation, the relationship was strengthened and there is greater trust today. Similarly, in my relationship with my best friend, Jessica, because of the psychological safety in that relationship, I feel safe to share whatever is on my mind or heart, so it's not surprising that I have grown immensely as a result of that relationship. For leaders, creating a psychologically safe culture not only creates an environment in which our team members are able to share openly, but also, it's the type of environment that is ripe for growth.

After all, organizations grow as a result of employee growth. It's the people inside of the organization that make the organization what it is. **Doug Bowen (Episode 040: Creating a Culture of Trust through Communication)** models that in the way in which he runs his organization, from the processes to his interactions and communication. Doug is the President at Bowen Engineering Corporation. Building off of the culture that his dad built, his concern for his team runs deep, as evidenced by the tears that were shed when talking about them. He shared a project in which his team members were working on a dam overflow. There was a man fishing with his waders nearby and got sucked into the water.

> **Doug:** *One of our carpenters ran out there and pulled the guy up the river. I get emotional because it means so much. One of our core values is genuine concern for other people. I hear about these things our employees do every day, and it humbles me so much to know that it's more than a paycheck. This is how people live their lives every day, and it makes me so proud to know that we really try to make this world a better place every day.*

It's no surprise that engagement is so high and turnover so low at Bowen. 40% of the company is owned by employees. Doug appreciates knowing that his employees bring an owner mentality to their work.

> **Doug:** *We typically tell clients that it doesn't matter where their project is located, or what the scope of the work is, odds are, they are going to have one or two owners in this company on their job site making decisions as an owner. Because of this, employees balance the short term and long term. We want to do a good job for the clients, so they will continue to have us back, and the shared ownership piece certainly changes the inputs that go into the decision that they're going to make.*

In building trust and an ownership mentality in his business, Doug has created an environment in which team members can be their best, and in Doug's story (as in all of the stories I've highlighted), trust starts with the leader and the choices that he or she makes. As my friend Tim Spiker says, "Leaders are able to be others-focused when they are inwardly strong." With vulnerability and openness, leaders set the tone for trustworthiness, just as Dennis Martin's story highlights.

Dennis Martin (Episode 010: Choosing to be Vulnerable) is the President, Individual Life and Financial Services at OneAmerica. He realized through candid feedback that he wasn't as ready as he thought for the position he desired. Dennis chose to lean into and embrace the feedback with vulnerability.

> **Dennis:** *Through the interview process, I got a lot of feedback and it was extremely humbling, but enlightening at the same time. So often when it comes to feedback, we're very naturally resistant to it because it's constructive or critical, depending how you receive it and how you choose to receive it. You tend to want to brush it off or push it away because you don't want to show that weakness or vulnerability because you're trying to get ahead.*
>
> *In reflecting on that time, I learned that the perception of me in a leadership capacity was much different than I thought I was projecting. I received a lot of feedback in terms of style and perception in what people thought of me and how I showed up. I just decided to take it and be vulnerable with it to see how I could adapt or think about showing up differently.*

Dennis says that he became very conscious of his impact on others and began thinking less about what he thought was right and more about what was happening with others. He softened his approach and began focusing on how to bring others in, helping to get things done to show that different side of his leadership. He says through that shift he received a lot of feedback about how he was showing up differently, and yet, he considers the changes he made slight course corrections. He calls them "behavioral shifts that had this massive impact on perception just because people saw that I was willing to change and adapt."

> *Dennis: It doesn't take a lot. Sometimes you will actually perceive that difference because it's the effort that people see. That made all the difference as I look back on the moment. And I think it was rooted in the fact that I really, really wanted the job, so I had the willingness to do what it takes. I started looking around and taking more people in. I very much have been a driver type, focused on getting things done, and now it is different.*

We are built to be in relationship, and our relationships are only as good as the level of trust that exists within them. As these stories highlight, trust is built over time with intentionality and vulnerability. My hope is that you are inspired to be more of YOU—real and authentic—in all of your key relationships.

COACHING QUESTIONS

- What is the level of trust and psychological safety in your key relationships?
- What strategy(s) will you try on to better leverage your key relationships?

9

LEADING UP

*T*hroughout the stories during the first year of *Being [at Work]*, the relationship theme emerged in story after story. It's important to note that it was relationships all around, in all parts of our lives, and in all directions (direct report, peer, and managers).

Gallup research indicates that 70% of an individual's engagement at work can be attributed to his or her manager. As I reflect on the jobs I have held, I certainly see a very strong connection between my level of connection and satisfaction and my relationship with my manager. It's a big driver of my passion for leadership development: bosses matter, but I also know that there is much outside of the boss's control. After all, it is a relationship, and each individual owns a huge portion of the relationship that he or she has with their manager.

How are you building and/or nurturing your relationship with your leader(s)? What I noticed in the themes across our guests' stories is a tendency to demonstrate the same important relationship-building behaviors with the leaders above us as we do those that report to us and that we work with.

The boss/employee relationship is the most important relationship in the workplace, so it's no surprise that it came up in these leaders' stories. Your relationship with your manager can make or break a work experience, no matter how much you love what you're doing. And just like any relationship, each person in the relationship brings his or her baggage into it, and each must do his or her part to strengthen the relationship. Of course, there is going to be tension and conflict because both boss and employee are human; both are flawed, both have strengths, and ultimately both want to be successful and add value.

While bosses have huge impact, I also believe that bosses get a bad rap. In a complex, dynamic workplace (and life), it's easy to blame the frustration or unhappiness we feel at work on our bosses. This talk runs rampant:

"I don't get enough direction."

"My boss doesn't appreciate me."

"My boss takes credit for the work that I do."

Imagine if we took all the time spent complaining about bosses and bottled it! That time adds up. Every second of time spent complaining about your boss (or anyone else) is completely wasted energy, and does nothing to help you.

Your boss is a human being, and gets tripped up just like you do. Reflect on the research I shared earlier—60% of managers fail in their first two years because they aren't equipped to manage—so your boss likely was not given much support or development when he or she became a manager. Why do we expect our bosses to have it figured out and to consistently lead us well? Just like you, your boss struggles with feelings of insecurity and doubt, and is going to make mistakes. By expecting your manager to keep you happy, you are setting everyone up for failure. Your boss does *not* have the remote control to your happiness and engagement—YOU do.

James Tanneberger (Episode 033: Leading Up: Strategies for Build a Stronger Relationship with Your Boss), President and CEO at SCI REMC provides insight on how best to lead up.

He was six months into a position at a municipal electric company when his boss left. Along the way, and actually as part of moving into this job, James had spent 18 years in business and had a lot of credibility in the places that he had worked. But when he moved to this job, he took on something totally different: Construction Project Management, which he had no background in. He was on the electrical side and didn't have the necessary construction experience.

> *James: I had a hill to climb, even from the doer perspective of building up credibility. With my boss leaving after only six months, I did not get an opportunity to interview for his job, and when he left, they backfilled his position with my peer, who had been there for many years. It was a little bit of a shaky ground for me. My new boss had a certain view of me because he had been my peer. And here I am coming into a role where I'm not as comfortable, so I'm not as much myself and learning at the same time, so he had a certain perception of me and my level of competence, so the relationship was a bit interesting at first.*
>
> *We looked at everything about 180 degrees different from each other. I'm a big-picture person who likes to have the vision of where things are headed and where they're going to be, and he very much approached things from a very detail-oriented view. This often led to us bumping up against each other because I was ready to move on, and he was slowing me down. We had our moments of friction early, and I had to make a decision. Is this where I want to be, long-term?*
>
> *I ended up staying seven years in this position — it was the greatest growth in my career where I learned how to lead up. By the time I left, it was a very positive situation because I learned to work with that leader and leveraged his*

characteristics that were 180 degrees different from mine. His approach to everything was different from mine, and I realized that gaining his respect and working together to produce a product that leveraged both of our strengths was the best thing for the organization. We got to the point where we were able to bounce back and forth and complete each other's sentences.

James emphasizes how he did this, and as you see from his example, it started with his mindset.

James: If the person who is leading you has good character, you absolutely can win in that relationship with them. You can get there. You can gain their respect, even if they look at things different from you. One thing I learned is to be loyal to your leader when you run into someone else. That way, your leader knows that you're speaking positively about them in every environment when they're not in the room. The next thing you know, they're listening to you. They're paying attention to your ideas. And what I also had to learn to do, because I didn't have a senior leadership title, was to be a leader in action.

I used my visioning strengths and learned how to communicate the big picture through *my boss, not around my boss, but through my boss and other people, so that they understood the vision and how they were going to help us. It became the idea of the group. Even though you don't have the title yet, you can impact your organization. Any time there was a chance to do something for another group that we had challenges with, like give the training that they needed for our federal regulations, I would volunteer to lead them in that training because I would build a relationship there.*

We had a program where you could write something positive that you had seen someone do in your group or in another group, and you could turn it in and they'd get a gift certificate. I used that to the fullest because I saw someone doing something good in another group. I used that to build a bond, to build a relationship.

An important note: There are situations in which bosses demonstrate dangerous or illegal behaviors. I am not addressing abusive supervision here. My goal in highlighting James's story is to address the common behavioral challenges that pop up in the manager/employee relationship and to encourage all employees to do their part to strengthen the relationship.

As an executive coach and leadership development facilitator, I spend time coaching leaders through challenges, and a common challenge to emerge over the years is the relationship with their managers. In most cases, when you feel disconnected, unappreciated, or frustrated with your boss, it's an issue of trust. Without trust, there isn't a foundation on which to build a relationship; so, my advice to anyone struggling in their relationship with their manager is to do three things to build trust in the relationship:

1. Soften your stance and focus on strengthening the relationship. When you're feeling frustrated, your guard naturally goes up. When you feel yourself starting to get frustrated, be intentional about staying open. Take deep breaths and speak slowly. If you truly want to improve your relationship with your manager, be intentional about going into your interaction with a more open demeanor.

2. Ask questions. As Abraham Lincoln once said, "I don't like that man, so I must get to know him." In order to build trust with your manager, you must understand him or her—get to know their style, preferences, motivators, etc. by seeking to understand. Your manager has a story—she or he has fears and pressures just like you do. By understanding those fears and pressures you are more likely to extend grace.

3. Leverage his or her strengths. We saw this in James's story with his boss who was so different from him. Rather than focusing on what your boss does NOT do, focus on the value that she or he does bring to your relationship. If you can't identify your manager's strengths, look again: everyone adds value in some way, and no doubt there is much to learn from your manager *if* your goal is to learn.

I've noticed throughout my career that when jobs got tough, I have tended to blame my manager. However, *I* am the common denominator in all of those relationships, so that pattern of frustration is on me. I could always point to a flaw within them to rationalize why I was struggling. And worse yet, I could talk to colleagues about their experience and really blow the manager's flaws out of proportion!

This is normal: we are hard-wired to self-protect by blaming others, so the important thing is to notice when you're doing it and shift our attention back to what we can control. Pay attention to what you're talking about, and if you find yourself complaining about your manager, stop and ask yourself what you can learn in the situation or reflect on why his or her actions are hurtful to you.

The best leaders are the best learners, and we can use the challenges that most frustrate us to grow and be better.

Yes, it's hard, but it's also a choice that you always have control over—are you going to choose to focus on what someone else is or isn't doing, or will you use the frustration to support your own growth?

Just like we've highlighted the importance of feedback in other stakeholder relationships, feedback is also an opportunity with those we report up to. When our leaders are demonstrating behaviors that are inconsistent with the culture they espouse, we have a responsibility to acknowledge that with them, to do our part.

Scott Zigmond (Episode 022: Leadership Creates the Culture) is a West Point graduate and the Vice President of Sales and Marketing at Performances Services. At a previous organization, his responsibilities were cut in half a few months after he came forward with some unethical behaviors he'd witnessed of his senior leader. He stepped up with integrity even though it wasn't recognized by others.

> **Scott:** *To use an old army term, you've got to have the intestinal fortitude to go talk to that senior leader and explain what you are observing or what your team is observing and why that's inconsistent with the culture. That's really difficult to do, to go talk to your CEO or talk to your V.P. or whatever, but if you're really bought into your organization and you are bought into your culture and you're seeing something that doesn't fit that from a senior leader, it is on you to go have that conversation with that senior leader, and if you don't, then that's on you.*
>
> *At West Point, we have an honor code that we will not lie, cheat or steal, nor tolerate those who do. If I saw someone cheating on a test and I didn't confront that person about that, I was as culpable as they were for cheating. We as leaders are culpable if we see a senior leader misbehaving and we don't address it. Now, I had this pretty interesting situation that happened some time ago, but there are little things that happen throughout the year that aren't as big as what I just explained in my story. Regardless of size or scope, you still have to have the intestinal fortitude to be able to go have that conversation. And if you tolerate it, then you've got to live with it.*

We can see through negative and positive experiences the value of trust and transparency in the relationship. **Brandon Brown (Episode 045: Transitioning to CEO and Replacing the Founder)** is the CEO of the Mind Trust. Brandon's pivotal moment in his career to date is the transition to CEO as he replaced the founder and throughout that experience, he learned the value of transparency and trust in the relationship. He highlights the things his predecessor did to set him up for success.

> *Brandon: He was very proactive in asking me what I needed to be successful. Through our very close working relationship, I felt the ability to be incredibly transparent with him and didn't feel the need to hold back. That then formed a strong working foundation for what our relationship would be like over the long term. I've had the ability to continue to value the rich history and traditions of the organization while making some very key changes and not feeling like I have to look over my shoulder to think, "What would the founder think of this?" I've had the freedom and the flexibility and the confidence from those around me to be really bold around not holding back when we think that some pretty big changes have to happen.*

The relationships strengthen us. They give us the courage to step out and take on the challenge. This is why peer accountability groups are so helpful when setting a goal. The feeling of being "in this together" strengthens our ability to move forward. Going big-picture provides the direction and the relationships provide the courage to step into and stay in the hard stuff.

As you'll see in the next section, the big picture and our relationships set us up to step into the hard stuff. In other words, we stay on the stage and keep going because it matters. We don't do it for the sake of doing it—if that were the case, we'd easily run off the stage, but because there's a foundation and a reason, we keep going and we step into the hard stuff.

COACHING
QUESTIONS

- What is your relationship with your manager (or leaders that you report up to)?
- What strategy(s) will you try on to improve the relationship with your manager (or leaders that you report up to)?

THEME III: STEP INTO AND STAY IN THE HARD STUFF

"Courage doesn't always roar. Sometimes courage is the little voice at the end of the day that says I'll try again tomorrow."

— *MARY ANNE RADMACHER*

10

ENGAGING WITH COURAGE

My stepson, Alex, struggled to adapt to online learning when schools shifted to a virtual classroom amidst the COVID-19 pandemic. He is a social kid and learns best when surrounded by his peers and with structure and encouragement from an in-person teacher. Caring a lot about his grades, my husband has struggled with how best to support him through it. He gets frustrated with Alex's lack of follow-through. He is a smart kid and does well when he does the work but getting him to do the work in an online environment has been a challenge. I have also struggled with how best to support him as his step-mom given that we are still building our relationship.

During one particularly challenging Sunday afternoon, when my husband realized that Alex was well behind and hadn't done anything to prepare for the upcoming school day, there was a big clash and many tears. I was doing my best to hide out in my office during the challenge, and as I was planning for my week and reviewing my bigger picture vision, I read these words that I had written in the family section of my annual goals: *"Grow my relationship with Alex. Encourage his schoolwork and activities he is passionate about. Be a soft place for him."*

With tears in my eyes, I recognized that hiding out in my office is not the demonstration of this bigger picture, so with a gulp and a sigh, I went to Alex's room and asked if we could chat. I asked some questions, acknowledged how cold it was in his room, and felt a bit awkward, but there I was, engaging because of the relationship I want to have with him. At the end of the conversation, I told him that I loved him and that I am here for him. It felt so good, even in the awkwardness, and it's good to retell and remember that moment as there are so many moments when I fail to do that. I take the easy path. I hope that it works out. This is why I spend time on Sundays in the bigger picture goals I have set for my life. They keep me honest and help to ensure that I show up in a way that is reflective of the vision I have casted.

Foundation gives us a safe place from which to take the leap. It provides courage to engage when we don't want to engage. Throughout the first year of *Being [at Work]*, leaders repeatedly shared stories of stepping into the hard stuff, and as I reflect on each of the stories in this section, I could also have used the stories in this section as examples for the first theme, go big-picture, and many for the second theme, focus on relationships. Our three themes are so well connected and supportive of each other—the big picture and the relationships give us the confidence to take the leap. It takes faith and courage to step into the hard stuff, and as these stories highlight, that is what great leaders do: they approach life as an adventure, with a growth mindset and a willingness to put themselves in tough situations.

Patty Hatter (Episode 017: Taking a Big Leap – What's the Worst that Could Happen?) isn't afraid to take the unfamiliar path. Throughout her career, she has jumped back and forth between operational roles, tech startups and for-profit board positions. The theme of figuring it out has been with her throughout her career. She asks, "What's the worst that can happen?" and this has led her to take some big leaps.

This pattern was set early in her career when she stepped up in a big way. She was working at Bell Labs, part of AT&T at the time, just out

of graduate school. Her boss had given her a lot of different opportunities, well beyond her years of experience while she was there.

> **Patty:** *I went into work one Monday and my boss says, "Hey,
> Patty, come in my office." He says, "I have a plan." I'm
> thinking, "Great, a new plan! This will be fantastic.
> Can't wait to hear it." We had been having success in
> driving bigger solutions, working with the AT&T sales
> teams in the US. And he says to me, "Hey, I want to take
> the success that we're seeing with what you're doing with
> the sales teams and driving these bigger, stickier solutions
> using very specialized skill sets. We need to start doing that
> in other markets. So here's my plan. You go to Europe,
> build that business, and then you come back. This is my
> plan."*
>
> *So I'm thinking, well, OK, I had two seconds to think about
> this. The sum total of my European experience had been
> four days in Munich on vacation, and that was it. That was
> the total time I had been in Europe up to that point. And I
> thought, "OK, we figured it out in the US. I'm sure we can
> figure it out there, even though I don't have any back-
> ground in the markets, and don't know how I'd find the
> sales teams to get in touch with the customers." But he has
> faith I can do it. I'm sure I could figure it out.*
>
> *And what's the worst that would happen is I get a great experi-
> ence in what it's like to do business in Europe. So this may
> be successful, maybe not, but I'll gain a lot of experience.
> So what is the worst that can happen? I'll raise my hand to
> this, and it ended up being such a transformational growth
> opportunity because it wasn't just going there with just a
> plan on paper. It's like: find the paper, find the pencil, start
> writing down the plan. How do I find these customers?
> What might they be interested in? How do I find the
> resources to deliver what they're interested in? And it was*

just taking it step by step, and after three years, we were able to develop so much business that was going well. We had three Bell Labs offices in Europe and the hubs where our business was most strong and then I was very much expecting to be coming back at that point and got convinced to sign on for another three years because AT&T was putting even more resources behind what we had done and the view was, "Patty you can't leave now; we're here to help. We'll be well. We're behind you now. Stay and help lift these even more." It was just such a great experience on multiple levels. You learn a lot from the roles that are the biggest challenge that you have. You learn a little bit of everything.

Similarly, **Kate Maxwell (Episode 050: Using Innovation to Engage and Highlight Team Members)** encourages her team to "raise yourself for the hard things." Kate currently serves as the Chief Technology Officer for Worldwide Defense & Intelligence at Microsoft. Throughout her career, she has put herself in situations where she is uncomfortable, and this has served her well.

Prior to her role at Microsoft, she served in a senior leadership role at Raytheon, and was the recipient of Raytheon Technology's Presidential Award for Driving Competitive Advantage as the founding director of a global innovation organization, which inspires and empowers employees to innovate across all functions and labor grades. She saw a need and she stepped up to fill it.

> **Kate:** *I was working in research and development at Raytheon, and I was not a huge player in the R&D scene. I was the process and execution lead. My job was to support all of the principal investigators if they needed something, so I oversaw their budgets and helped them with procurement and supply chain if they needed materials for research. I loved that job. I had the privilege of seeing all of these good ideas that would bubble up each year related to research and*

*develop the things that we could be working on as a
company to set us up for success in the future.*

*I would see those ideas come through, month after month and
year after year, and they were awesome ideas, but there was
always this concern that it was many of the same players
and innovators bringing those ideas time after time. I
thought, surely there are other good ideas out there. We
have people that work in secure areas, locked away all day,
working on things that are classified, so they don't get to
get out and maybe speak to their colleagues in other loca-
tions or working on unclassified programs. We have new
hires and interns by the tens of thousands that are fresh out
of school and are probably bringing bright new perspectives
to our company. What if those folks have ideas, and they
just don't know how to either connect the dots or bring
them forward to the leadership they are connected with?*

*So I took that idea to others. There was this need that existed to
go find and capture all the other good ideas that were out
there. A small team of us that were working in the research
landscape jumped on this idea and banded together. It was
the power of the collective, so to speak.*

*We got our little innovation squad together and we put a busi-
ness case on paper and we went to the research and development director and said, "You know, Sir, we want to find
a way where we can communicate innovation, and why it's
important, out to the company, out to the masses. We want
to educate more people about what innovation looks like at
Raytheon Technologies, and how they can get involved.
We'd like to have a little bit of seed funding set aside so if
somebody has a good idea, they don't have to go through all
of the process associated with getting a multibillion-dollar
budget."*

> *Good ideas come from everywhere. We were granted that initial budget to prototype and innovate and disrupt the business itself in some ways. We got started. We started hosting innovation brown bags and lunchtime topics, and teaching people about how to bring forward their ideas. We started providing feedback and coaching the people on how they can connect their ideas with business value, because in a business that's really how you advance something: you show the company how it could have a return on the investment they're going to make in that idea. This caught fire in a way that none of us expected.*

Kate's story is an important one for emerging leaders who often discount their perspective with all kinds of limiting beliefs: *I have not done this before; I don't know what I'm doing.* The truth is, none of us *really* knows what we are doing, so why not share what you're thinking?

I once worked at a security company, supporting hundreds of field-based leaders. I worked in the corporate office and the sales managers I worked with were based in sales branches across the country. The success of these sales offices was driven from the leadership in the branch, so my primary role was equipping these leaders to be successful. With my team, we dedicated our time to looking at the system in which they were leading, providing the support they needed, and helping to remove obstacles, but one thing I failed to consider early on was the way in which they were compensated. Because they were accountable for sales, a big portion of their compensation came from the sales commission they earned each month through the sales advisors on their team.

There was a separate team within the corporate office that administered the commission, and fortunately for me, one of them sat in a cubicle right outside of my office. My perception of Veronica was that she was quiet and kept to herself, so I could tell she was a bit apprehensive when I first approached her to learn more. As I began asking questions, I very quickly realized that we needed to connect the dots between the work that Veronica was doing and the work that my team was doing, as there was evidence in her work that pointed to some clear gaps in the work we were doing.

As I began to work with and learn from Veronica, my perception of her quickly changed—she was incredibly vocal, with all kinds of great ideas. She simply had never been asked to share her opinion. She worked as part of a team in which the leader literally worked all day behind a locked door and was not open to ideas or opinions, but once the floodgates were open, her work became an important part of the work my team was doing. We began collaborating and included her in our weekly meetings with field sales managers to ensure they experienced the connection.

This experience taught me to pay attention to the expertise and insight that team members have, and not wait for them to come forward, but instead, create an environment in which others feel safe to share their opinions and perspectives. Veronica sat outside my office with all of this information that was so helpful to our team. We only needed to tap into it, and I'm so glad that we did. It's also encouragement for all team members to step up and share their perspective, as you never know where that might lead.

Melissa St. John (episode 042: Will Your Office Space Need to Change Post-Pandemic) is an example of someone who shares her perspective for the benefit of all. Melissa is the CEO and owner of Relocation Strategies. The company was founded by a man named David Baize – Melissa had worked with him as a vendor and was impressed with David and the organization, so she went to David and shared this.

> *Melissa: I told him, "I want to join your team," and David's response was "Absolutely." I literally started on the same day that the conversation began. It just came to me that I wanted to work with him. We worked very well together, so I started with him and immediately and pretty quickly told him that we needed to redo all of our marketing material, and he just let me do it.*

Then, fast forward, and it's no surprise to me at all that he tapped me on the shoulder and asked me to consider buying the business. I didn't even let him finish the sentence. I said yes because I know what I want. And I wanted it.

It filled my heart with so much passion because I was advocating for all these clients. We were helping them with their relocation, with their offices. We were designing it. We were bidding out furniture, getting them good pricing, so I purchased the company and it's just been a wonderful opportunity to be the captain of my own ship and recruit team members and move forward. I've owned the company now for 14 years. If you're really passionate about the work you do, it's just not work.

I appreciate these stories of bold women stepping into the challenge. I'm beginning to embrace the challenges in my leadership more and more as they are opportunities to rise and learn more about myself. Early in my career, I let moments of "I have no idea what I'm doing" terrify me. Those moments would stop me in my tracks, and today, I am getting more and more comfortable moving forward with the fear and doubt. I am not going to let the fear stop me, just as it did not stop **Natalie Wilkinson, (BONUS episode: Trusting Yourself)** the General Manager of Corporate Strategy and planning for Toyota North America.

Before I share Natalie's story, I must share a personal note about our relationship. Natalie is the *Being [at Work]* guest I have known the longest—almost 30 years. She is my sister-in-law, and one of my all-time favorite people. She was the first guest on the show; when the head of our production team asked me to identify an initial guest, she provided some key criteria: someone you know well (to ensure good communication flow), someone you respect, and someone who has a good story to tell. I immediately thought of Natalie.

In almost 30 years, I can honestly say that never once, not one single time, have I ever heard her blame or complain. She leads with humility, positivity, and a focus on the solution.

Natalie has spent her career at Toyota and now leads as an executive, having experienced tremendous growth through her tenure with the organization. She highlights her mentors and sponsors as being pivotal in her career and nudging her to take the big leap. When approached about a stretch position, she was full of doubt.

> **Natalie:** *I hired into a production control position and managed a small group of about 10 to 12 specialists, professionals in an office environment setting. I was approached as a career growth opportunity to rotate from that comfortable environment I had been in for seven or eight years. I had done most of the jobs in it and knew most of the ins and outs of what each person was doing every day to move to the production floor and manage 400 people in one shop, which is where they actually assemble the metal body of the vehicle. There are about 400 people, 24 hours a day, seven days a week, and about 700 robots to manage. I had grown up in the production control world, so when I was approached with this opportunity, the very first thing in my head was:* "There's no way I can do this."

However, she thought about it a lot, and she talked to her mentors and sponsors (which she is so grateful for). She says:

> **Natalie:** *It took me a couple months to actually make that decision to step out of that comfort zone. It was a lot of discussion with both my mentors and my sponsors to build my own confidence, to leap out there and say,* "YES, I can manage a group of engineers. I can lead 400 people to build bodies every day."

> *I didn't think I could. The first reaction I had was there is no way, and then I found a way. It took several months. I*

know there were a couple of moments when I thought "What am I really getting into?" and what I realized is your management style is your management style, no matter where you're doing it and what size group you're doing it for. As long as you put people first, focus on development, and focus on improving people's work conditions, you're going to be successful. YOU don't have to be the expert as long as know how to DIRECT the experts.

Building on the foundation of their values, stepping into the hard stuff involves leaders going against the grain and following their own path. In each of these stories, as in Natalie's situation, these leaders made the choice to engage.

Lisa Price (Episode 014: Making Decisions that are Right for You) is the Chief People Officer at KAR Global, a global 1000 company of complementary businesses that provide support, technology and logistics for the used vehicle industry. In 2005, Lisa was serving as an employment lawyer and an opportunity emerged to explore an in-house legal position. She was eight months pregnant with her first child and was contemplating introducing another big change from a career standpoint, so it wasn't a decision she made lightly. Her colleagues' flat out told her that she was making a mistake moving into the corporate setting.

__Lisa:__ It was a lot of weight. I needed to make the best decision for me from a career standpoint, knowing the family situation was following either way. Making that decision to leave the partnership track to go in-house, for me to get over that hurdle, I really felt I had to embrace change, not view it as limiting or scary, but instead more opportunistic and see what was behind that curtain, to see what was next.

A lot of times, we're very quick to question ourselves: "Can I do that? Will I be successful at that?" But really, __the courage to make the choice is leadership__. You make the

*decision, go all in, take that chance, even though it's not in
your comfort zone. Go for it. That's what I did in 2005 and
I am super thrilled to say I'm still working in that
corporation.*

**Melissa Davis's (Episode 016: Laying the Groundwork for Your
Future)** example also serves as an important reminder to know and do
what's best for you (as that will ultimately be the best for all). Melissa
is the past President of BSA LifeStructures, an organization she chose
to step away from for six years to support a family need.

> *Melissa: I worked as an interior designer for 15 years and left
> for a brief period of time to spend time with an ill family
> member who needed caretaking. I came back in the role of
> the Director of Interiors for the firm and at that point in
> time, we had three offices. We now have six offices, and we
> grew in that period of time when I was Director of
> Interiors.*
>
> *While I was gone, we were left without an Interiors depart-
> ment, so when I came back, I basically had to start the
> group from scratch. We had two other people that were here
> besides me that had been part of the previous Interiors
> group, and the three of us together built the group back up
> again, hired more amazing people and grew the group to
> over 20 people across all six offices.*
>
> *I guess I did something right in doing that because it got the
> attention of the chairman of the company. The chairman
> felt that it was time to bring in new blood and we were
> lacking a bit in the area of culture, so the chairman felt very
> strongly that we should bring in somebody that had a focus
> on the culture of our firm. He approached me and asked me
> what I would think about being the President of the
> company, so I went from being an Interior Designer to
> being the Director for the firm to being the President of the*

firm nationally and had absolutely no idea that that would ever happen in my life.

Never be afraid to do what works for you at whatever point you are in your life, because YOU CAN. I know a lot of people are afraid to step away because they feel like they can never re-enter back in. I'm an example of the fact that you can come back after doing what you need to do for your family and your personal life, and come back to even bigger and better things.

The common thread in these stories is the importance of speaking up: just as Mayson recited every word of her assigned poem many years ago (while her little voice was shaking), leaders must speak up and advocate for themselves and others.

Kevin Brinegar (Episode 049: Putting Your Name in the Hat) is the CEO of the Indiana Chamber of Commerce. Many years ago, he made a courageous decision to throw his name in the hat for the position when it came open. During the interview process, he made it clear to the search committee that he wanted the job.

Kevin: The search committee was formed, and it was pretty stiff competition. There were three or four individuals who were already heads of other Indiana associations, as well as some national candidates. The search committee set up an initial interview, via video conference, and then, they narrowed the field down and presented a group of six to eight candidates to interview with the search committee. The intent was after the first interview, they would narrow the field down to two or three finalists and then they would do a second interview and then make the selection.

During my interview with the selection committee, I outlined my passion for and knowledge of the chamber and the vision I had for the future. At the end, they asked, "Is there anything else you want to say?" I thought about it, and did something that ran counter to my coaching and my under-standing of what you're supposed to do in interviews. I was sitting at the end of a conference table and they were around the table and I looked at them and pointed my finger pretty sternly and said, "I just want you to know I want this job." And those were my last words.

I felt comfortable that I would get through that first cut and would be part of the final interview, but then, something unexpected happened. The next day, I got a phone call from the search committee chair. She said the search committee had discussed the interviews with all of the candidates and they've decided to forego the second round of interviews and offered me the job. Wow! That was one of the best phone calls I ever received.

Kevin did what he felt was counter to his coaching – he assured the search committee with 100% certainty that he wanted the job. Stepping into the hard things means going against the grain because your heart and desire is pointing you in another direction.

Jim Piazza (episode 005: Making Unpopular Decisions) went against the grain and made an unpopular decision early in his career. Jim is the Director of Data Center Operations at Facebook. His pivotal moment occurred at a previous organization early in his career, when he was asked to do something contradictory to his values.

Jim: The word came down that we were going to have to start doing layoffs. Reductions in force carry a slew of not only legal and company requirements, but then of course there's the personal aspect of it. We got into a room together with our HR leadership and they hadn't developed any talking points. I had only been managing for a couple of years at this point so I wasn't experienced and the sales vice president said, "We need to develop what we're going to say." And I agreed, that yes, we absolutely DID because we were about to make a major reduction in force.

The sales VP then said, "We'll tell them that things just couldn't be better." I paused and I said, "What are you talking about?" And they said "Well, you know, we have to give them some hope and we have to tell them that this is for the survival of the company and the rest of the employees."

And I said "Hold on a second. I completely disagree with this approach. You're taking something that is going to affect people's livelihood and going to affect the way that they're putting food on the table for their family and the way that they're making their mortgage payments and the way they're supporting themselves and you're trying to turn it into something positive when it is NOT"

It was a really unpopular thing to say. I had to make a decision, and just prior to saying that I had to pause because I could have said one of two things: I could either 'toe the company line' and say "Okay, sounds good," or I could do what I knew was right in my heart. I couldn't get behind trying to paint this off as something positive when it's not. These were people that I had been arm in arm with at 2 o'clock in the morning in the data center, pulling cable for the next customer that's coming in, and ordering pizza, and working really hard to make sure that we were hitting our customers commitments. How could I possibly look these people in the eye and say things couldn't be better? I couldn't compromise what I believed just because it was the easiest route to take. It just wasn't who I am, and to this day, if I was put in the same situation again, I know I would do the exact same thing.

Mona Euler (Episode 025: Go After It and Believe in Yourself) is the Founder and President of My Healthcare Advocate, an organization she founded. Prior to starting her own business, she spent 14 years as the CEO of Kindred Healthcare and she talked about the journey that got her to that position. Her belief in herself and going after what she wanted were both a big part of making that happen.

> **Mona:** *I don't like people telling me I can't do something, especially when I think I have the experience and confidence. You can believe in yourself and still have that drive to do what you need to do. Seize opportunities as they come, even though you are scared. After I'd been at Kindred Healthcare for about a year as the Director of Case Management, I was really enjoying the job and was still learning, and then they were creating a chief operating officer position at that time. I thought I should apply, and it was an incredible opportunity, so I did and got the position.*
>
> *I was in that position nine months when the CEO position became available. This was big. I was confident, but I was scared. I was pretty young at that time, twenty-nine years old, and I remember them asking me why I wanted the job, and the first thing out of my mouth was "Because I think I can do it." They had flown in an individual from the east coast, and he was going to interview me for an hour and then he had to go to the airport, so I sat there in my suit with butterflies in my stomach and he proceeded to talk for 45 minutes about himself and about the company.*
>
> *I realized that he was going to leave and not know that I really wanted this job, so I stopped him at about ten minutes until he was to leave and said, "I don't mean to be rude, but I really have something to say. I want to make sure you know that I can do this job and why I can do it before you leave." I remember his mouth sort of dropping down and he let me talk about my abilities and what I was going to do in that role, and I did get the job. I got that CEO job, and that was a pivotal moment for me, because I was the youngest person to become a CEO, and the first female.*

Donna Wilkinson (Episode 008: Modeling Risk Taking) is also a great model for risk taking. Donna leads HR at Pacers Sports and Entertainment.

> *Donna: Being an athlete, I look at risk in a different way. I have learned that you can't grow unless you're out of your comfort zone. Risk sounds negative, but I'm more of an optimistic type of person. I've been drawn to challenging situations.*
>
> *The two industries that I selected and ended up working in for most of my career are the meat business and sports. The funny thing is that there traditionally haven't been a lot of female leaders in those industries. When I look back at the biggest challenge in my career, I think "What was I getting myself into?" 17 years ago, there weren't a whole lot of women in leadership roles in sports, in any sports because it was just a tough business. We work when people play, and there are a lot of rigors and demands. It's not very family-friendly, but I've wanted to change that as I was one of the very few women in an executive position who were in a dual career family.*
>
> *I have had the privilege of working around amazing trailblazing women at the Pacers—Kelly Krauskopf who is our assistant GM who built our Fever and is the first female basketball General Manager in the league. Mel Raines who leads our facility is one of only four women who leads the facilities in NBA arenas and is president of our all-star initiative and that has helped our momentum. The fork was taking a leap into this environment of sports. Because we have such great owners and supportive leaders, it's been a challenge, but we've been able to really do some cool things here and allow for a lot of growth. Our goal is to be the best place for women to work in sports.*

Donna's story connects the dots between the foundation of the big picture and stepping into the hard stuff. Her mindset around challenge and risk has put her in the position to step into and stay in the hard stuff. Her sports examples are relatable. I played volleyball and tennis all through high school and when I reflect on the matches and games that stand out to me, it's the ones in which we took a risk, tried something new, and defied the odds.

In any pivot or challenging moment, we have a choice—the choice to engage or the choice to pull back—and in the moment of choice is our power. What will you choose?

COACHING
QUESTIONS

- What holds you back from making the choice to engage in tough moments?
- What strategy(s) will you try on to build your courage and confidence?

11

STAYING IN THE HARD STUFF

*B*ecause of my love for volleyball, several years ago, I raised my hand when an opportunity arose to coach my daughter Mayson's team. It was the 7 and 8 year old team and the first time Mayson had played. Because many of the girls had not played previously, we spent much time on the basics—learning to pass the ball and getting the serve over the net. We also had a lot of fun and named ourselves "Team Awesome."

Several of Mayson's closest friends were on the team, so I knew them and their parents well, which helped to shorten the learning curve. Talent emerged, and it became clear who our best team members were and who struggled. My daughter, Mayson, was one of the smallest (and youngest) on the team, and while we worked and worked on it, she could not get a serve over the net and didn't want any help from her mom. I realized quickly that it was going to be a tough season. Fortunately, I had a co-coach who focused on helping Mayson, and I went to work focused on where I could be most helpful.

At the end of the season, we participated in a tournament with eight other teams. We had talked a lot throughout the season about having fun and learning (those were our two primary goals). As the girls talked about winning the tournament, there was a shift, so I acknowledged with them that we had been having fun and learning and asked them what the goal was for the tournament. They all yelled "win." I told them that because our goal was to win, we might have to make hard decisions, and it was important that we were all supportive of that, and they all agreed.

We won our first two games in the tournament, and advanced to the semifinals. There were just four teams remaining and the girls were pumped up. The first few points in the first game of the match went back and forth—we were tied at 13-13 (playing to 15 points). It was Team Awesome's opportunity to serve, and Mayson was up as server (who to this point had still never gotten a serve over the net); she grabbed the ball with a lot of gusto and started to head back to the service line, and I called time-out to substitute in a better server. Mayson was devastated. She took a seat at the end of the bench with her head down and glared at me. The substitute server, meanwhile, scored two straight points and Team Awesome won the game 15-13.

Substituting in a better server (knowing that my daughter would be so bummed) was an easy call for me to make because we had decided as a team that we wanted to compete—we wanted to win—and we had all agreed on that. That alignment gave me the courage and confidence to make the tough call and to lead through the repercussions.

It's one thing to step into the hard stuff with courage, but it also takes discipline to stay in it, and to follow through.

My husband and I work hard to engage in the conversations that trip us up the most—conversations about finances and step-parenting. Both topics are emotionally triggering for each of us in different ways, so I often avoid the conversation, but when I engage in the conversation with courage and stick with it, sharing honestly and with openness, I am always better for it. I literally tell myself in the tough moments: *"Lean forward, stay in it, and LISTEN"* as my tendency is to flee. I want to get to safety, but that doesn't get me to clarity—fleeing keeps me in the chaos, so I remember: Mayson recited the entire poem on stage many years ago. She stayed in it. My husband and I completed the 14er. We stayed in it.

As I reflect on the stories from the first year of *Being [at Work]*, I am struck by the strength of our guests not only to engage in the challenge, but to stay in it. Their stories provide the key for HOW to stay in, and how to best lead through a challenging moment.

Britni Saunders (Episode 021: Driving Change in a Traditional Organization) is the previous Director of the Indiana State Personnel Department. She was appointed to the position by the governor, aligned with his mission of taking Indiana to the next level. Her mission was to transform the employee experience for thirty thousand employees statewide, and the leadership challenge was a daily, personal one for Britni. According to her, listening, curiosity and openness to conflict are the key leadership skills when driving change in a traditional organization.

> *Britni: I have learned to be a better listener, and I have learned to appreciate the hard work that has come before me. It's easy to walk into a new place and say, "Hey, I've got all these great ideas and let's do them," but it's harder to see what has been done before you and to appreciate the privilege that you have to make this amazing fun stuff happen because of the hard work that came before you. That's something that I didn't always do well here, but that I learned how to do better, and I think that's helped make me successful.*
>
> *It's a trendy thing to say, but it's critical to have a genuine sense of curiosity. It's hard to actually do that at times because it may lead you down paths that you didn't want to go down or to conclusions you didn't want, but it has served me well. And then the last thing is: being okay with having a very loving sense of conflict, which sounds like an oxymoron, but I have a guilty pleasure for being able to ask the question that I actually want to ask and not feeling like*

I can't have the right conversation at the right time. I've practiced that a lot. It's hard in government especially, and other, similar organizations in which people have done something a certain way for a long time, and there's probably a lot of good reasons why they've done it that way for a while, and then there's another group of people who say, "Well, you don't have to keep doing it that way. Let's think of all these innovative ways to think differently." And those perspectives are both really important. If you can figure out how to marry those up, then you have the best of both worlds. You learn from the past and are able to make an educated decision on how to prepare.

As Britni's story highlights, being open in the conflict takes maturity and integrity. When we do so, connection and growth happen. I have struggled with commitment in all aspects of my life, and a direct challenge is that I am not good at staying in an argument. I want to yell and scream and get the heck out of there, and yet, each time my husband (or team member, or anyone in my life for that matter) and I work through a conflict, we emerge stronger as a couple. Knowing this and getting it builds the confidence to *stay in it.*

Being willing to stay in the conflict also involves the acknowledgement of how you are feeling. While I am an expressive, encouraging leader, I am not good at acknowledging my feelings. I am a thinker—always thinking—so I often "think" my feelings rather than actually feel them.

Recently, my daughter Mayson reminded me of this. We were preparing to host a party in our home—all day, I had worked to prepare the food and décor to ensure that everything was perfect for our evening. Fifteen minutes before the party started, my husband came home, and in that moment, I realized that I had not gotten myself ready for the party (and had flour from baking all over my jeans), so I was short and curt with him, and ran upstairs to find something to wear. My daughter, Mayson, knowing me well, grabbed a couple of things from the closet for me to put on, as I frantically brushed my hair and freshened my make-up. In my hurriedness, she grabbed me and said "Mom, take a minute to let it out and feel what you're feeling." I told her that I did not have time for that and that I needed to get downstairs, and she asked me the question that I most needed in that moment, "What is going to serve you best in the long run?"

Karen Mangia (Episode 013: Success with Less: Making More Time for You) was forced to explore this question. She learned the value of saying no. Sometimes the hard stuff that leaders have to step into is saying no, or not me, or not now. Karen is the vice president, customer and market insights at Salesforce. She knows something about leading a very full calendar. She is the author of an empowering book called Success with Less. She reached a point many years ago when she could no longer ignore the signs that she needed to slow down and focus more on her needs. Today, Karen is intentional about taking care of herself so that she can best serve others.

> **Karen:** *The story of the pivotal transformation in my life could be summed up with really a three word story:* Yes. Never. Release. *Those three words became very powerful stories with a lot of context in my life. Along the way of a career climb and all of those fantastic career opportunities, I noticed over time I wasn't feeling quite like myself.*

> *I think we all have this inside voice that talks to us from time to time, and it doesn't always say super convenient things. Usually that inside voice is telling us that something is out of alignment. Maybe we're not happy, or not healthy. We're not feeling well. We need to make an adjustment, and more often than not we cover up that inside voice with activity because it's a little scary to be quiet and to reconcile with what might actually be going on. And in my situation, I was noticing that as I was making some great career progress, I was starting to feel really tired and not just the kind of tired where you didn't get enough sleep last night. I mean a bone-deep, no matter how much you sleep, kind of tired, but I explained it away a little bit.*

*And then I started gaining a little weight. I thought, we all do
that. It's age related, or because I'm traveling so much; it's
easier to eat those delicious appetizers and desserts at the
restaurant, so I thought, well, maybe I'll just start going to
the gym a little more instead of working on email during
that period of time.*

*Eventually, there was a powerful attention-getting moment for
me. I went to make a phone call to my brother and when I
picked up my phone, I realized I couldn't remember his
name. Now, here I am at 33 years old. I have one brother
and we talk to each other every week. And one of the things
I realized is a powerful one word story I was telling myself
in those early years of my career climb, was that the only
word that really mattered, that equated with success, was
the word* Yes.

*I grew up in a house where I didn't have, and wasn't neces-
sarily surrounded by, a lot of professional female role
models. When I came into the workplace, I took a combination of what I did growing up, the chore chart kid who got
the gold stars and checked things off and got approval for
doing those right behaviors, and combined it with what I
thought I saw other successful people doing at work. I
thought what they did was they always said yes. They
delivered results and made it look easy, and the reward for
that was getting more.*

*That compounded into a major medical issue to the degree that
I went chronically undiagnosed for three and a half years.
As my hair fell out, my skin turned gray, and my eyes even
changed color at one point. It was so alarming. After
getting a correct diagnosis three and a half years later, it
still took another five years to get well from that point. And
of course, it was alarming to me, staring out on a horizon
where the story I was telling in my head was that next*

powerful word: Never. *I started to think to myself: I'll never be healthy and I'll never be successful, because what I have learned over time was the formula for success was saying yes and doing more. I hit the point where that was no longer sustainable. It was a really alarming feeling, to not only be sick and not know what that meant for my longer term future, but also to know the way I had gotten to the point I had in my life and my career literally could not continue.*

That's where my story enters the third word: Release. *I had never had such a clear sense that I had very limited time and limited energy. I needed to be much more diligent about where I was spending that time and energy. I had to learn techniques to release obligations that no longer served me to make room for people and experiences that did. That became the genesis for me starting to understand that people who are amazing leaders are, by the way, people who really enjoy their lives and lead fulfilling, happy, healthy lives without saying yes to everything. Instead, they set a goal. They understand what success looks like for them, and they make choices about whether the time and energy they're spending is moving them closer to those goals, or further from those goals.*

I found it challenging to learn those lessons publicly as people watched me grow ill and struggle to be the person that they engaged with for so long. It was a really transformative time in my life, though, to have that discovery. I'm grateful I had it at a time in my life when I still have many more years ahead of me to work, and hopefully to live a full and happy life, because that lesson about release is so powerful and has made it possible for me to not only have great experiences and be healthy, but also more importantly, to enjoy them.

Karen's story is another reminder of the strength in having a strong foundation. Early in her career, Karen put her strength in the success, not the foundation of who she is as a leader. At one point during our conversation she said, **"You've got to get to know who you are without the busy."** What a great suggestion—*who are you without the busy? Behind the activities and deadlines, who are you? What's your driving force? Why are you doing what you are doing? Are you reacting to it or responding based on your values? Are you living by default or by design?*

Your essence knows the answers to these questions, but the big loud world blocks the answers from emerging, so we must stay close to and protect the still, small voice within. **Our inner wisdom is so much smarter than our ego,** but we can only hear it when we get quiet and shut out the noise around us. By practicing this, we learn to pay attention to the intuitive nudges—that's how I think of my internal wisdom, as it shows up in all kinds of situations.

There was a particularly full season in my life recently and suddenly I found myself double-booked for two client engagements. As soon as I discovered this, I jumped into my natural problem-solving action mode, looking at colleagues' calendars to see who could help, preparing a communication to the clients and to team members to engage them in helping.

Just as I was about to hit send on an email to a team member (which would also have whipped her into a tailspin), I felt the intuitive nudge: "This is not going to help. Be patient. It will work itself out." My ego fought that guidance, as I wanted to figure it out now, but I honored the guidance (a bit painfully) and literally within a few hours, two clients reached out needing to shift dates freeing up my schedule, and just as my internal guidance had suggested, it all worked out.

Responding instead of reacting is the key. Taking it in, acknowledging what we're feeling, considering the bigger picture, AND THEN responding (and maybe choosing not to respond at all). My step-daughter, Sophie (who is wise beyond her years), is someone who demonstrates this well. She has an uncanny ability to connect with the feelings of others and communicate back to them what they're feeling in a disarming, helpful way. She speaks her truth and allows others to speak theirs without getting sucked into being right or having to prove herself. She is grounded in who she is and let's others do their thing. She is riding the waves of life, and while she has strong opinions, she doesn't get tripped up by what's happening with others.

Life is made to work out—I wholeheartedly believe that because **it always has**. Yes, it is full of ups and downs, but at the end of the day, there is a bigger plan unfolding. My part as a leader is to engage with life through my bigger picture perspective, stepping into situations with faith.

Notice the connection to the first theme of going big picture. This is an important distinction—these leaders did not step into the hard stuff for the sake of it; they did so because of a bigger picture perspective, something more important and because of the people around them. This is when you can trust your actions—when it's coming from your bigger picture values and vision for the common good.

Throughout this theme of stepping into and staying in the hard stuff, we have been reminded how to do that from the stories of several leaders:

- Own and communicate your perspective . . . It's YOURS!
- Be bold in sharing it.
- Trust yourself.

Early in my career, I struggled to build a relationship with a team member. Her leadership style was very different from mine—while I am naturally a dreamer and see the possibilities, she naturally pokes holes and is skeptical, so I perpetually felt like she was crushing my ideas. She led a significant part of our business, so I knew it was important to build a relationship, but in hindsight, I went about it all wrong. I focused on the "easy" team building efforts. We had a shared vision that we were aligned on, we worked through some tough situations together, but for a long period of time, my focus was on the results she was getting which impacted the level of trust she had in me and our relationship.

Rather than asking questions about her and how she was doing, my questions were focused on the client work she was engaged in and her sales activity. For a long time, I did not take the time to get to know her and ended up making a lot of assumptions.

There was a pivotal moment in which we spent time together personally. It was a turning point as I saw a completely different side and it was an opening to a new relationship. While her skepticism continued to fly in the face of my optimism (and always will), I learned to appreciate her and our relationship in a new way, because I got to know her as a person.

The bigger picture provides foundation and encouragement, stepping into and staying in tough situations moves us forward, but without the relationship, there is no meaning. And BECAUSE of the relationship, it's worth it to stay in the tough moments.

COACHING QUESTIONS

- What keeps you from staying in the tough moments?
- What strategy(s) will you try on to better navigate tough moments?

THE POWER IN THE PIVOT

"There are moments that define our existence, moments that, if we recognize them, become pivotal turning points in our life."

— C.W. GORTNER

1 2

IMPLEMENTING A FOUR-STEP
VISIONING PROCESS

*S*ince I can remember, I have enjoyed making up stories in my head. As a kid (actually this is something I still do), I spent hours imagining the possibilities of what could be: seeing myself on stage, meeting the President, becoming an astronaut, traveling the world. I would fall asleep creating stories, seeing all kinds of fun, future events.

I enjoy thinking about the future. It gives me energy. Today, as a business and community leader, parent, and wife, the thing that keeps me grounded and focused is the vision, the possibilities that exist. In other words, the bigger picture is the glue that keeps me going—it is my safe place to fall, and often, I fall on it hard. It provides clarity amidst the uncertainty, something to cling to when I'm looking for some sense of assuredness. It is a representation of my faith and belief that life is working with me.

Throughout this book, we have seen through the stories of many leaders, the power of a bigger picture.

In this chapter, I outline the 4-step visioning process I have used for many years. I have shared this with hundreds of leaders over the years and have noticed three typical reactions:

- **I'm in:** *"This is great. It forces me to take a step back and reflect on where I'm going. I'm looking forward to reflecting on these questions."* Typically, this reaction is from individuals who share my enjoyment of thinking about and reflecting on the future. They are big-picture thinkers naturally, so this process feels empowering and affirming to them.
- **I'm in, but it will be hard.** *"This is hard, but I know I need to do this."* Typically, this reaction is from goal-oriented leaders who recognize the potential and opportunity before them, but they often get hooked by obstacles or things they cannot control. They tend to be more past and present oriented, so thinking about the future does not come naturally.
- **I'm not in.** *"This is interesting, and I can see the value in it, but I would never take time to do this."* I have facilitated development programs for over 20 years and have always appreciated the saying, "When the student is ready, the teacher appears." So much of our growth and development is about timing and what's going on in our heads and hearts. For this group, I encourage them to explore the process and then follow the steps that will be most helpful to them.

Regardless of your reaction, I encourage you to explore the process and see what insights emerge for you. It can be a process to follow in its entirety or to pull pieces from. I also encourage you to engage those closest to you in the process as appropriate. For example, this is an incredibly helpful process for partners or spouses or families to engage in together to create a shared vision for their lives.

Taking the time to step back and reflect on what it is you want is the first step, but there are two guiding principles that support the process in its entirety. Think of these guiding principle as foundations for this process:

Principle 1: Belief in the power of a bigger-picture vision. It's much easier to say NO to something when you have a bigger YES. During my tenure at a previous organization, the leader gave each team member a clear binder that did not have a cover so that you could see through it. The first page included a place to note your "Top 3 Priorities" to ensure that your focus was always top of mind. I appreciated this practice, and it became a habit. For the last several years, I have used a clear binder and the first page in the binder is a document that I refer to as "My Leadership Focus" (I will share more about this tool and how it's used in step 4 of the 4-step process.) At the top of "My Leadership Focus" is my vision and values to provide visibility and something to filter my choices through. My belief in a bigger-picture vision guides the choices I make every day.

To "go big-picture," you must have a bigger picture to go to.

Principle 2: Belief in the power of my thoughts. What I THINK ABOUT is shaping my reality. A few years ago, my parents were visiting, and I was looking forward to a relaxing day with them and my husband. It was a beautiful spring day and I imagined us going exploring, shopping and having a nice meal. It was just the four of us as our children (we are a blended family) were with their respective mom and dad. We were lounging around that morning, drinking coffee and tea and my husband announced that Sophie (his oldest) was running a 5K with her mom and that we should all go. My parents immediately jumped in, saying they were all for it and that they would love to see Sophie.

My reaction, however, was not a positive one. I thought to myself, "This isn't the day I had planned," so I took that negative attitude into the day and my experiences reflected it. Just before the race was about to begin, I recognized that I was the one creating the problem, based on how I was reacting, so I literally went into a port-a-potty (to get some privacy) and said a prayer. I acknowledged that I was reacting immaturely, that I was with my husband and parents (just as I'd wanted), and it was an opportunity for me to show support to my new stepdaughter and to my husband. I got myself back into a good headspace and then, I rejoined the group. Immediately, I felt lighter and the sky seemed brighter. We had a delightful morning, cheering on Sophie, and then went exploring and had a great meal.

The key in this story is that I recognized that it was *my* reaction that was shaping the situation. I am grateful that I recognized it, otherwise I could have easily slipped into a victim mentality and ruined a perfectly great day with my parents and my husband. Many people are living by default, *reacting* to whatever comes their way. I fell into (and continue to fall into) this trap. Each of us has an opportunity to be intentional about *responding* to unwelcome circumstances and shaping our experience in the process. There is a big difference between reacting to something and responding to it.

In 2007, as part of a coaching certification program I participated in, I was required to read the book, *Breaking the Rules: Removing the Obstacles to High Performance* by Kurt Wright. The book changed my life and completely shifted the way I think about goal setting. It deeply resonated with my inner visionary and provided the foundation for a visioning and goal-setting process that I now use with clients, and in my own life. It is my system for living my life on purpose, with intentionality. It is the system that helps me to respond to situations versus react to them.

Through the encouragement and insight in the book, I created a 10-year vision for my life in 2007 over the course of a few weeks. At that time, I was single (three years post-divorce), working for a consulting firm, and trying to figure out how to balance a full consulting career while raising Mayson (who was five at the time). In trying to make these parts of my life more of what I wanted them to be, I reacted a lot to situations: unhealthy relationships, doing work that I shouldn't have been doing, and compromising precious time with Mayson in the process. I dreamed of more, so I allowed myself to imagine the possibilities of what could be for my life. I knew there was a deeper longing within me, so I wrote down what I wanted based on questions from the book. I created a vision board based on what I had come up with, and I talked about my vision while expressing gratitude for all of the good in my life. I wrote these three statements into my 10-year plan in 2007 and 10 years later, in January 2017, I experienced the reality of each of these (just as I do today):

- I am happily married to a beautiful man who encourages the best of me. We are co-creating a brilliant, bold life together.
- I lead a growing organization that is modeling the way for leadership and talent development.
- Mayson is 15 years old and such a bright light in my life. She is confident and has a strong faith. We laugh a lot and talk about everything.

By going out ten years into the future (beyond obstacle thinking), I was free to imagine the possibilities that most spoke to my heart. These realities were very important to me, so I gave them plenty of airtime and focus. I believe (from this experience and many like it) that what you think about, comes about. The results you get are ultimately born in the thoughts you have. Too often, our dreams and ideas remain as lofty ideals. Without focused attention, they are unlikely to come to fruition. So instead, we go through our life *"hoping for the best"* and *"waiting to see what will happen."* A much more empowering approach is to create a plan and take ownership for working towards those things that are most important to us.

An example that many of us can relate to is setting a weight loss goal. I will stress again the sentence in the last paragraph—a much more empowering approach to goal setting is to create a plan and take ownership for working towards those things that are most important to us. And yet, most people set goals from a place of unhappiness—*I am not happy with how these jeans fit or how I look in the mirror, so I'm going to lose weight.* Clearly, that approach is doomed from the beginning, because it is starting from a place of ick.

Just like this example, the majority of individuals approach the goal-setting process backwards which hinders success; setting goals for the next week, one month, three months, six months, one year, etc., continually keeps us focused on the obstacles in our current state. In other words, setting goals for next week, one month, three months, etc. keeps us stuck in the muck of what is. This hinders our ability to "get on a roll" and as feelings of disappointment and lack emerge, our goal setting falls apart and we don't accomplish what we set out to.

To "get on a roll" and feel inspired and motivated around accomplishing our goals, we must extend our thinking out beyond the obstacles—to where our minds are suddenly set free to think ideally. Research shows that it takes most individuals 7 years in the future to no longer see obstacles, so I suggest ten years into the future as the *starting point* of the 4-step visioning process. It looks like this:

STEP 1: CAST A LONG-TERM VISION

What if there were no obstacles? If you had a magic wand to create the life of your dreams, what would you do? What does the horizon of your life look like? Which relationships are most important to you and what do you want them to look like in ten years? These questions are the spirit of this first step. This step encourages you to dream, stepping out of "what is" and into "what could be."

We are dynamic, complex people and there are many aspects of our lives, so it is helpful to think holistically. Wherever you go, there you are. Each part of our life impacts the other, so when going big-picture, it is important to explore all aspects of ourselves—our spiritual life, our family make-up and the relationships within our family, our career lives, our social life and the relationships we have with our closest friends, our health and our financial picture. These six areas form the general categories in which to explore; name them however works best for you. After all, this is your future vision, so align the nomenclature to your picture of the future.

I was recently working with a coaching client to support her transition into a new role. Thinking about the future is challenging for her (as it is for many). She does not get energy from dreaming about what could be, and as we were beginning to explore a vision for her new role, she said in frustration, "I am not good at this and can't come up with the vision."

After validating the challenge in the process, I encouraged her to give herself grace and to take it one step at a time. Rather than jump to having a vision, I asked her if she had the energy to answer some questions. She said that she did, so I asked her what it was about this new role that was different from what she had done before. I asked her what came to mind when she thought about what she would be doing in the new role. I asked about the people that she would be working with and what they would be doing. As we explored her unique image of this new role with different questions, the picture started to get clearer.

When casting a long-term vision for our lives, it is helpful to think of it as a process and take it one step at a time, enjoying the exploration along the way. For each of the six categories noted previously, there are questions that will help you formulate your longer-term vision of the future:

Spiritual

- What does my spiritual life look like as I view it ten years from now?
- What actions am I taking on a regular basis to review and enhance my spirituality?

Family

- What family relationships am I focusing on 10 years from now —what do those relationships look like?
- In what special ways are the lives of those closest to me reflecting the love and support I have given them?
- In what kind of special activities am I regularly engaged with my family?

Career

- Thinking ideally, how do I see myself earning a living in ten years?
- In what ways is this allowing me to achieve my fullest potential?

Social

- In what kinds of social activities am I regularly engaged as I view myself ten years from now?
- In what clubs or organizations am I actively involved? How do I describe my circle of friends?

Health

- In what kind of physical shape am I as I view myself ten years from now?
- In what kind of exercise programs am I consistently active? How do I feel about my health?

Finances

- How much money is required on a yearly basis to fully support the above activities?
- As I view myself ten years from now, what is my overall satisfaction level with my financial picture?
- What progress have I made toward accumulating wealth for my future years?

STEP 2: SET GOALS

You know the drill – a new year comes upon us, and leaders from all walks of life begin looking to the new, setting goals typically based on what they want to change in the new year—what they are currently unhappy with. According to a study at the University of Scranton, 92% of new year resolutions fail by January 15 because of the motivation behind the goal. Most individuals set goals backwards. Instead of projecting an image of how they want the future to look, they react to goal setting because of something they don't want or like in their lives. This is why setting goals is not the first step in our visioning process.

First, we go big picture because that is when we get out of obstacle thinking. Obstacles to achieving exist in the mind and it is these obstacles that keep us from accomplishing our goals because they keep us stuck in the muck of what is, and this is why so many goal-setting efforts fail.

Once you have a longer-term vision, you can set goals from a place of motivation – you are in a good position to "get on a roll" and can ask yourself, "what do I need to accomplish in the next year to make progress towards the long-term plan?" Based on your long-term vision, identify annual goals in each of the six areas. In other words, what do you want to focus on in the coming year to propel you in the areas of spirituality, family, career, social, health, and finances?

As I said earlier, the aspects of the vision I created in 2007 that I focused on, came to be. Those that I had the most passion for and spent the most time on came to be. When you set annual goals or shorter-term goals, it is helpful to be disciplined in two ways.

First, set a focused number of goals. I suggest no more than 2-3 goals for each broader category. In the book *The Four Disciplines of Execution*, the authors share research that highlights the importance of narrowing your goals to focus on the most important priorities. The more goals you try to juggle at once, the less likely you will be to reach them.

Second, set goals that you are passionate about. Without energy and attention, your goals won't have momentum and it will be tough to get on a roll. If you don't "feel it," don't include it in your goals.

As an example, here is the long-term vision and the annual goals for the career section of my plan. 2020 was an unpredictable year, as we all know, and yet, the focus and energy around the three goals I set moved me closer to the long-term vision. Notice that the annual goals are focused (there are three of them) and they are all things that give me a lot of energy.

10-Year Career Vision

- I have the freedom to choose work and adventures that most inspire me.
- I lead multiple organizations and initiatives, teaching and speaking all over the world, lighting the way for others.
- The *Being [at Work]* brand is a leader in leadership growth and intention (podcast, annual conference, books, journals, etc.).
- The Next Gen Talent brand is a leader in the development of early-career talent (running in 10 markets, over 1,000 leaders participating in multiple industries).

Annual Career Goals

- Prepare to scale and replicate Next Gen Talent in new markets and into other industries.

- Build on the momentum and success of Being [at Work] — new guests in new markets!
- Write and publish leadership book.

STEP 3: BRING THE GOALS TO LIFE

The next step in the process is to bring the goals to life in some way – create a visual representation of your goals. Once you have a focus for the year or the short-term, determine what it looks like. The most effective way I have found to do this is to gather images that reflect my goals and paste them onto a poster board. Some call it a dream board and others call it a vision board—regardless of what you call it, the key is to see the goals. If you can see it in your mind's eye and feel it, it can absolutely be yours! While you can certainly create a vision board for your long-term vision, I encourage you to focus on the upcoming year (or short-term goals) and have fun in the process.

There is an old saying that serves as a good reminder: It's not enough to stare up the steps; you actually have to step up the stairs. In other words, your vision is only as good as your willingness to take action on it. Creating a visual representation helps to bring the goals to life so that they are more actionable.

We see in pictures – taking the words on the page and transforming them into powerful imagery. An image increases memorability and makes the invisible visible by creating a visual representation of an intangible object. Here is some additional guidance based on a process that has worked well for me and many others:

After you have created your goals for the upcoming year, look through magazines or search online for pictures/images that represent your goals. After you have collected several (at least one for each goal—remember, no more than 2-3 goals for each area in your long-term vision), paste them onto a poster board. Have fun with it—there is no way to mess up your vision board because it is yours. The keys are to ensure the goals are aligned with your long-term vision and that you feel passionate about each of them.

After you've pasted the images onto your poster board, find a spot in your home or office to display your vision board. Make sure it is visible everyday so that you have a daily reminder (and a picture) of what you are creating.

Vision Board Party 2019 — Equipping these emerging leaders to go big picture! (Upper from left Emily Sorg, Mayson Moore, Cassandra Williams; lower from left Alexandra Reed, Zoë Franz)

This is also an incredible way to engage your kids or kids in your life in the visioning process. There is a group of friends who have adopted this practice since our kids were young. Many years ago, my friend, Janet, hosted a vision party for our group and for many years it was tradition, as we met in early January. We spread out all over her living room with our magazines and our poster board, scissors, and glue, and start perusing images. The kids always enjoyed the creative process and proudly displayed their vision boards at the end of our time, talking through their big dreams for the year ahead.

As the kids have gotten older, I've noticed how their futuristic thoughts are maturing. In 2019, as juniors in high school, they were starting to set their thoughts on college and beyond, so going big picture equipped them to think longer term, an important skill they will leverage throughout life.

STEP 4: INTEGRATE THE VISION INTO YOUR LIFE

There are two specific ways to integrate the vision into your life: 1) Use the vision to focus your time and energy and 2) talk about your vision.

How do you determine what to focus on throughout the day? Are you living by default, reacting to what pops up, or are you living by design?

Living by design takes discipline and intentionality. It's much easier to say no to something when you have a bigger YES. And, a long-term vision and goals serve as a very strong yes. The key is to identify a rhythm in which you review your vision and goals and then align them with your choices and what shows up on your calendar. Discipline and intentionality are personal, so determine a system that works for you.

I have found a weekly rhythm to work well for me. It fits into my life and work. Each Sunday, I spend about 10-15 minutes reviewing my long-term vision and my goals and then I ask myself, "What three things am I going to do this week to move closer to the vision?" Those three things become my "top 3" priorities for the week, and I track them in my leadership focus tool (sample below). Then, each morning, I do the same thing, and I ask myself, "What are the top 3 things I am going to do today to accomplish my top 3 for the week?" The vision and values don't change – they are the constant ensuring that each week I am spending time on the activities that matter the most and are most fulfilling.

At the bottom of my leadership focus tool, you'll notice that I also spend time each Sunday and each weekday expressing gratitude. Expressing gratitude softens my heart and reminds me of the blessings all around me. It creates a spirit of appreciation for all that I have and the new things I am creating. For me, it is a critical part of this practice. It also balances the drive and ambition that comes with working towards goals.

Leadership Focus Tool

My Vision/Top Priorities		My Core Values	My Strengths

Week/Day	Week of:	Monday	Tuesday	Wednesday	Thursday	Friday
My Top 3:	1. 2. 3.	1. 2. 3.	1. 2. 3.	1. 2. 3.	1. 2. 3.	1. 2. 3.
What I'm Grateful For:						

Another way in which you can use your vision is to talk about it. Share it with others. What you talk about, you give energy and attention to. Share your goals with your family (or better yet, do the process together), your friends, and your colleagues. Talking about your vision for the future is always uplifting—it will not only inspire your goals, but it will most definitely inspire others to be more intentional with their lives as well.

The vision also becomes a place in which to respond in challenging moments. Rather than reacting emotionally, imagine asking yourself *"how would the '10-year vision version of me handle this situation?'"*

No one can go back and make a brand-new start, but anyone can start from here and make a brand-new end. Regardless of the tool, template or process that you use, take time to create a vision and focus for your life. Otherwise, you will spend your time reacting to whatever it is that comes your way. With a plan and focus, you can create the life you want.

Exploration mode can be both exciting and scary. These are questions regularly rolling around in the heads of many leaders: *Where am I going? What do I want? What might it look like to try something new? Is it time for me to do something else?*

During a recent conversation, a friend who is in exploration mode expressed that she was ready to leave her current role and was looking for similar ones. Having known her for a long time, and knowing that she had a passion for politics, I asked about those aspirations as she also has expertise that would support her in that arena. She agreed that, yes, she had always dreamed of a career in public service, but didn't think it was practical right now. Then she said the words we've all heard and said many times: "Maybe someday…"

And that is perfectly acceptable if that is what is best for her right now, but the challenge there is that if we continue to push things to "someday," we will never see those things come to be, because someday is not an actual day. It is an indefinite time in the future, so it is helpful for leaders to push a bit when others talk about doing something *someday*. In this situation with my friend, I asked what small step she could take to explore that right now, given that she's in exploration mode, and she identified a couple of things quickly.

Ron Atchison was a Canadian football player who was known for his toughness and durability. He once said, "If there is something special you want to do, now is the time… if you want to make a difference in the world, now is the time. Don't be fooled into thinking you should wait until you are older or wiser or more 'secure,' because it doesn't work that way. The wisdom will come. The security will come. But first you must begin your adventure."

Beginning the adventure is the key: what small step might you take towards that thing you've always wanted to do someday? Rather than waiting for the right time, go for it! Why not? Isn't it all one big adventure anyway?

Someday is not an actual day; if there is something you really want to do someday, empower yourself to take a step in that direction. I'm hopeful that the steps and tools I've shared in this section are helpful starting points.

13

STAYING ON THE STAGE

I have a big, bold faith in life. It serves me well as a leader in all aspects of my life. I know that life is always working with me, so I ride the waves of life with my bigger-picture dreams and goals providing general direction, BUT I have no idea what's around the bend. I don't need to because I trust life. The bend wouldn't pop up if it weren't helpful in some way. I may fly out of the lifeboat, or the boat may be turned upside down along the way. I will emerge with bumps and bruises, but I will have great stories to tell and will learn something in the process. As my writing coach, Dr. Adrienne Maclain says, "it'll either be a good time, or a good story!"

The same is true for you and all leaders. No one is immune from challenge. My pastor says that God is much more interested in my character development than he is my happiness. Through each challenge, I am learning. When pivotal moments emerge, I go big-picture, leverage the relationships, and step into and stay in the hard stuff to get from chaos to clarity.

Throughout this book, as I've unpacked the themes that showed up in our guests' stories, I have shared stories and situations throughout my career. It has been such great fun to reflect on my own growth and pivotal moments. I remember in my first job in Chicago going to lunch with my friend Jamie Banks (who is a rock-star in the eCommerce space). Jamie and I couldn't wait for our lunch hour; our favorite lunch space was the Thai place down the street from our office. We would laugh about the silly things we experienced at the office and complain about the frustrations, the disappointments, and the tensions. So many of those challenging situations remained unresolved because we ran off the stage. I ran off the stage over and over again. I didn't give feedback to the leader who bullied me. I didn't share what I really thought about the direction the team was going. I didn't share information with colleagues because I wanted to be the one to present it to the boss. I didn't share what I was really thinking.

It's not that I am regretful—I don't look back now and pontificate on what might have been. Instead, I use these situations as fuel for the challenges that pop up in my life today, because I recognize the lack of growth in NOT stepping into the hard stuff. I believe (who knows for sure, but I do believe this to be true) that, faced with those same challenges today, I would lead differently because of life experiences. I AM leading differently today because of my growth. Because we each lead from the essence of who we are as a person, we cannot separate our growth as a person from our growth as a leader. Just like we are all growing as people (we can't NOT grow in the process – that is why we are here), we are always growing as leaders.

Today, the challenges look a bit different, but they are always there, just waiting for me to lean into them. And once I do, and I've grown through them, life will bring a new set of challenges. We rise and we fall. We succeed and we fail. We feel bad and we feel good. **Who do you want to be through it all?** That is a big-picture question that will serve you well, because you get to decide who you want to be through it all. You are in the driver's seat when it comes to how you will lead through the challenges you are faced with. Every. Single. Time.

So, who do you want to be through the challenging times in your life? You get to choose. It takes discipline to keep the focus on the bigger picture and the relationships and not get hooked by the stuff of life, so it's important to step back and remember that life isn't happening to you. **Life is happening through you.**

Yes, no doubt there will be wonky times, but why ruin a perfectly good challenge by calling it "bad" or "awful," when in reality, IT JUST IS. Like any challenge, the situation is completely neutral; we make it what it is by how we think about and talk about it. Of course, I would have loved to hug my parents on Thanksgiving 2020, but because of the pandemic, we chose to stay home, and my husband and I had a quiet day and a great Thanksgiving meal, and I got to try something different. My mom always makes the turkey, but in 2020, I got to – I brined it and it was so, so good! I was glad to get to try something new. Later that evening, I got to hang out with my daughter Mayson and her friends: we had a dance party in our kitchen and facetimed with family. That experience represents who I want to be through challenging times: an adventurer exploring new territory with enthusiasm and some dancing along the way.

Pay attention to what YOU are making of the challenges. Pause and reflect on how you are talking about and thinking about the challenge. It's all happening through you. By taking responsibility for the meaning you bring to whatever it is you are going through, you are empowered in the process.

Go big-picture, focus on the relationship, and step into and stay in the tough moments. **What a great way to take care of yourself and each other.**

GRATITUDE

Thank you for being on this journey with me. We are in this together, so let's continue the conversation. There are several ways to stay connected:

- Follow me (Andrea Butcher) on LinkedIn and Facebook.
- Follow HRD – A Leadership Development Company on LinkedIn, Instagram, Facebook, and TikTok.
- Subscribe to *Being [at Work]* wherever you get your podcasts.
- Participate in a public leadership growth experience. You can learn more on our website at https://hrdleadership.com/.
- Please review the book and share key takeaways. How are you more empowered to lead through the pivots in your life?

Finally, my greatest request is that you always take care of yourself. YOU are a once in a lifetime historical event. What an honor that is, so please do the work of discovering who you are and what makes you tick. That is the best way to serve yourself so that you can serve others.

I wish you all of this with much love,

Andrea Butcher

If you enjoyed this book, please leave a review on Goodreads.com or on Amazon at amzn.to/3LRIHh1.

ABOUT THE AUTHOR

Andrea Butcher is a catalyst for growth. Wherever she goes, she brings light and encouragement to the people she serves.

Andrea is a visionary and leads organizations and teams from big picture to execution. She is a dynamic speaker, certified executive coach, and facilitator. As the CEO of HRD - A Leadership Development Company, she drives the organization's growth strategy. She also hosts the popular leadership podcast, *Being [at Work]*.

Andrea's work spans organizations of all sizes and industries all over the world; she has experience in global HR positions, consulting, operations, and executive roles for private and public organizations.

She is also the co-founder and President of Next Gen Talent, a program specifically designed to equip emerging HR leaders for success.

Andrea is married to Robert Butcher and together they enjoy all kinds of activities and adventures. They are both life-long learners and enjoy traveling and new experiences. As a blended family, they have three kids—Mayson, Sophie, and Alex—who bring so much joy and growth to their lives.

https://linktr.ee/andrea.butcher

ABOUT THE PUBLISHER

RED THREAD PUBLISHING GROUP

Red Thread Publishing is an all-female publishing company on a mission to support 10,000 women to become successful published authors and thought leaders. Through the transformative work of writing & telling our stories we are not only changed as individuals, but we are also changing the global narrative & thus the world.

Visit us at:

www.redthreadbooks.com

facebook.com/redthreadpublishing

instagram.com/redthreadbooks

Made in the USA
Columbia, SC
25 October 2022

70027334R00107